Multiculturalism in Indian Fiction in English

Multiculturalism in Indian Fiction in English

Ashok Chaskar

ATLANTIC

PUBLISHERS & DISTRIBUTORS (P) LTD

Published by
ATLANTIC
PUBLISHERS & DISTRIBUTORS (P) LTD
7/22, Ansari Road, Darya Ganj, New Delhi-110002
Phones : +91-11-40775252, 40775214, 23273880, 23275880
Fax : +91-11-23285873
Web : www.atlanticbooks.com
E-mail : orders@atlanticbooks.com

Branch Office: Chennai
Phones : +91-44-48531784, 28291383
E-mail : chennai@atlanticbooks.com

Printed & bound in India by Atlantic Print Services

Preface

Literature is a social discourse which needs to be studied from different perspectives and points of view as each literary text more or less encompasses the panoramic view of human society. Most of the literary scholars and students prefer to analyze or study the literary texts by applying different theories and premises and follow the long-established ways of analyzing texts.

The present book is an attempt to analyze the selected Indian novels in English by applying the theory of multiculturalism—an emerging social theory which has acquired wide range and scope in the fields like politics, sociology, anthropology and literary studies. It is a social theory that recognizes and respects minority cultures which have been suffering from social injustice, exclusion, marginalisation, dispossession, dislocation and social discrimination. It also explores the possibility of breaking down inter-ethnic, inter-racial discriminatory attitudes, cultural jealousies and supports the maintenance of social harmony and acceptance of all cultures. In a sense, multiculturalism opposes cultural hegemony and respects all cultures with their distinctiveness. In writing this book, I have tried to promote the value and significance of multiculturalism in literary studies. An attempt has also been made to analyze the novels in the light of infringement and carrying out of the principles of multiculturalism in the selected novels.

I wish to express my deep indebtedness to Dr. Simon Bernabus, whose kind inspiration and encouragement made me to undertake this project. I also wish to express my deep gratitude to all the friends who have directly or indirectly helped and encouraged me in writing this book. Last but not least, I thank my wife, Shobha and son Aditya for letting me concentrate on my work. I would also like to thank Atlantic Publishers and Distributors (P) Ltd., for bringing out the book in good quality and design.

The book will be useful to the students and teachers of English literature, Indian English literature, particularly fiction, and researchers in these fields.

Ashok Chaskar

Introduction

This book aims at exploring how multiculturalism, as a social theory, functions and plays a vital role in literary studies. Multiculturalism is not a single school of thought emerging from a single discipline. It has acquired wide range in literary studies. As a social theory, multiculturalism brings together different themes such as cultural diversity, recognition, mutual concern, peaceful coexistence of many cultures and subcultures. It promotes the value of social heterogeneity—an essential part of human life, and respects minority cultures that have been marginalized for centuries. Multiculturalism opposes cultural imperialism and compliments all cultures with their uniqueness. In a sense, it challenges the monoculture society and celebrates cultural pluralism. The coexistence of numerous cultures and subcultures can build up a healthy human society characterized by cooperation, tolerance, respect and love. The idea of preserving all cultures is a way of recognizing different cultures and representing them as equals in the public arena. The preservation of different cultures leads towards the integrity of society. Though multiculturalism opposes cultural hegemony, it appreciates cultural diversity and respects the notion of multiple identities at individual, cultural, ethnic, religious and national levels.

Recognition is central to multiculturalism. Recognition may be of different kinds—community recognition, group recognition, gender recognition, etc. Multiculturalism as a social theory recognizes and respects minority cultures that have been suffering from social injustice, exclusion, marginalisation, dispossession, dislocation and social discrimination. It explores the possibilities of breaking down inter-ethnic, inter-racial discriminatory attitudes and cultural jealousies and supports the maintenance of social harmony and acceptance of all cultures.

The book attempts a close examination of four Indian novels in English: *Untouchable* (1935) by Mulk Raj Anand, *Train to Pakistan* (1956) by Khushwant Singh, *Bye Bye Blackbird* (1971) by Anita Desai and *The God of Small Things* (1997) by Arundhati Roy. However, all principles of multiculturalism are not equally reflected in all the novels.

The first chapter, "Theoretical Framework", begins with an analysis of the multi-layered term 'culture' and its diverse range of meanings. The anthropologists and social scientists have various definitions and consequently, there is no monistic view of culture. Rather, it encompasses the whole way of human life. It is very dynamic, progressive and interactive. Though the term culture is slippery, in the present book, the aim is to define its social dimensions rather than its different implications in various disciplines. Like culture, literature mirrors different cultural traits, social institutions, stratifications, power structures and power relations of a particular society. Any literary text more or less tries to discover the whole panorama of human life with its similarities and differences. This chapter therefore, traces the postcolonial theory and its impact on a newly emerging theory of multiculturalism. The principles of multiculturalism include peaceful coexistence of many cultures and subcultures, concern for minority cultures, equality of rights and equality of opportunities. However, the chapter closes with a detailed survey of Indian multiculturalism, as it is reflected in the selected Indian novels in English.

The second chapter, "Multiculturalism in *Untouchable*", is a comment on certain prevailing social facts in Indian society. Bakha, the protagonist of the novel, suffers a lot due to the existing caste system, poverty, oppression, social injustice and exploitation. He tries to protest against the upper caste Hindus, the members of a dominant culture, but fails in his mission to shape an egalitarian vision for himself. The rigid caste system in India has created social inequalities and injustices. Particularly, the untouchables, members of the minority/subordinate cultures are purposefully kept away from the mainstream society, where the power structure is determined by the 'highborn'. In the name of purity and pollution, the upper caste Hindus make untouchables economically, culturally, socially and politically powerless and weak. Though the Constitution of India has provided the blueprint of an egalitarian society, in the novel, the so-called dominant culture systematically sidetracks the minority cultures and pushes them to the periphery. Multiculturalism always helps to challenge the dominance of one culture over the others and protects the idea of equality of opportunity and equal rights to the minority cultures. However, in the novel, instead of granting opportunities and rights, the minority cultures are inhumanly victimized and oppressed by the dominant culture. Throughout the novel, the sharp rift between the dominant and subordinate cultures promotes social disharmony and disrespect in the village, Bulashah.

The members of the minority cultures like Bakha are always deprived of their basic rights. Bakha does not get an opportunity for education because of his social marginalisation. Therefore, he is forced to do menial work which often demoralizes and disheartens him. Ideologically, multiculturalism and democracy are very close to each other, as both concepts promote equality of rights and non-discrimination. But throughout the novel, the members of the minority cultures remain passive and inactive due to the pressure of cultural dominance, exploitation, oppression, social inequality, injustice, caste discrimination, intolerance, socio-economic marginalization and subordination.

The third chapter, "Multiculturalism in *Train to Pakistan*", begins with a social and political history of pre- and post-partition India. The novel portrays pre- and post-partition life at the frontier between India and Pakistan that had become the scene of rioting, violence, brutality, cruelty and bloodshed. The communal synchronization and harmony were scattered after the partition by a series of tragic events. For the sake of interpretative convenience, the novel is analyzed along two separate lines. The first line involves a pre-partition period in which the principles of multiculturalism are carefully and visibly fostered. People of different communities, religions and castes are seen maintaining their socio-cultural harmony and peaceful coexistence. The Sikhs, Muslims and Hindus in Mano Majra make a positive contribution in solidifying a cultural mosaic in Punjab. They respect each other's religious, cultural and linguistic practices and encourage differences in terms of food habits, lifestyles and beliefs. They mutually accept each other's religious differences and practices with respect and love. Their positive approaches to socio-cultural and religious diversity extend their sympathies and deepen their self-knowledge. Their socio-cultural harmony and peaceful coexistence illustrate a slogan of multiculturalism, i.e. 'living together separately'.

The second line focuses on the post-partition period in the novel which is marked by discrimination, dislocation, displacement, disintegration, doubt, hatred and loss of human values. It also echoes the rise of destructive communal and religious identities, which break down the socio-cultural harmony and peace of Mano Majra, a miniature version of India after partition. The evil consequences of partition are seen in the post-partition Punjab, where partition creates a wave of communal hatred. Though partition is a political decision, it disturbs the social harmony and peaceful coexistence of the masses. It separates people, uproots them culturally and socially. It creates a wave of socio-cultural disharmony, communal jealousy and a sense of insecurity. The principles of multiculturalism are visibly violated in the post-partition Punjab.

The fourth chapter, "Multiculturalism in *Bye Bye Blackbird*", presents Indian immigrants' problem of acculturation in England/Europe. The novel, *Bye Bye Blackbird* unfolds issues like racial discrimination, cultural alienation, East-West discord, identity crisis, intercommunity/interracial marriage, racial prejudice, cultural dominance, cultural rootlessness, xenophobia, social ostracization and socio-religious conflict. The major thrust of the novel is on the continuous oscillation between Oriental (Indian) and Occidental (British/European) culture. The Oriental culture is seen as traditional and spiritual, whereas the Occidental is more materialistic and modern. The Oriental culture is more accommodative and, occasionally submissive, and its accommodativeness and submissiveness are easily reflected in the behavioral patterns of the Indian characters in the novel. On the contrary, cultural superiority of the Occident is seen through the western characters who try to maintain their centrality and cultural dominance over the 'other' subordinate (minority) cultures. The Occidental colonizers' negative attitude towards Oriental culture is seen through their linguistic and cultural dominance. Therefore, though immigration is primarily an economic phenomenon, it has socio-cultural dimensions also.

Adit, the protagonist of the novel, is initially fascinated by the British culture. His love for Occidental culture is exemplified in his love of English society where there are employment opportunities and social liberty. But after his marriage with Sarah, a British girl, he realizes the true colours of British culture which he has been admiring. He has to bear many racial insults and humiliations inflicted on him by his in-laws and others. The cultural rootlessness he experiences in Europe and a sense of alienation make him return to India, a multicultural home. Sarah, Adit's wife, tries to absorb cross-cultural shocks of dispossession and humiliation. Her marriage to a native East brings a sense of cultural insecurity and alienation. In England, in her own country, she is not at peace. She suffers from social ostracization only because of her voluntary acceptance of an Indian culture. Actually her marriage to Adit is a positive step towards recognizing other cultures. But the so-called Occidental (superior) culture treats her as a social criminal. Sarah's association with Oriental (Indian) culture and her decision to move to India are not only a sign of cultural assimilation but also recognition of the 'other' culture. Sarah is a cultural ambassador who is trying to pass on a real message of multiculturalism.

The fifth chapter, "Multiculturalism in *The God of Small Things*", reveals the socio-cultural, religious and political setup in Kerala society in the latter half of the 20th century.

The narrative revolves around the Ayemenem house. The older members of the Ayemenem house are more conservative and have nurtured their brutishness, pretensions, egotism and male chauvinism. Though multiculturalism embodies the principles of equality, freedom, justice and human dignity, the so-called upper caste, dominant patriarchal culture bluntly violates all these principles and controls the power structure of society. Throughout the novel, minority cultures become the victims of injustice, exclusion, marginalisation, dispossession and discrimination. Ammu's intercommunity love marriage is a right step to bridge the gap between cultures and communities. But the dominant patriarchal culture is not ready to recognize and accommodate such amalgamation. Her strange behavior is one of the signs of her growing rebellious spirit against the dominant patriarchal culture which discards and neglects her. As transgressors of 'Love Laws' both Ammu and Velutha have made an attempt to develop their own 'subculture', but the so-called proponents of the dominant culture do not allow them to establish their 'subculture'. The policy of multiculturalism promotes the value of equality and justice to all groups and cultures, but in the novel, the principles of multiculturalism are brutally violated by the dominant patriarchal culture. Throughout the novel, the members of minority cultures become victims of different forces like poverty, casteism, tradition, social taboos, politics and bureaucracy. Under the disguise of caste and cultural superiority, upper caste people treat lower caste people as their slaves and make them mentally, socially, economically and culturally weak and fragile. Arundhati Roy has made an attempt to highlight the need of establishing a peaceful society—where everybody's interests, rights and cultures are protected and respected—for strengthening the principles of democratic multiculturalism. But the novel ends on a tragic note shaped by injustice and unfairness.

The concluding chapter sums up the ideas and points emerging from the issues discussed in the preceding chapters, which are essentially my own findings. It states my conclusions concerning the positive/negative reflections of multiculturalism in the selected novels. I have attempted to show how multiculturalism, a social theory/ideology, helps to maintain social health through mutual respect, love, tolerance, acceptance, recognition and accommodation of different cultures. The focus is on the social facets of multiculturalism. In the selected novels, multiculturalism is manifested in different forms. But all the principles of multiculturalism are not equally seen in all the selected novels. The present study is just a step towards underscoring the significance of multiculturalism in literary studies. The study concludes with an emphasis on the importance of multiculturalism in literature, a discipline which effectively deals with the multiple dimensions of human existence in society.

Ashok Chaskar

Contents

1

Theoretical Framework

Culture: Nature and Scope

Culture is one of the most stimulating and motivating subjects of study in academic circles. It includes anthropology, history, literary studies, sociology and politics. Culture is a slippery but a comprehensive and inclusive term. It is not born or created but it evolves and grows. Therefore, its scope and relevance are not clearly defined. It is often used as a synonym for 'the social' because it is social in nature. It is a way of life, a set of values, beliefs and behaviours that makes one particular way of life distinguishable from another. The meaning of culture in social science is broad enough to include all human traits and social structures which are learnt and not innate. In general non-innate traits are assumed to be different in various societies and the variations contribute to the formation of multiple cultures.

The term 'culture' has a complex, multifarious history and diverse range of meanings in contemporary discourses. Different anthropologists use it differently. E.B. Tylor was the first 19th century anthropologist to define and make extensive use of the term. According to Tylor (1891: 18): "Culture is that complex whole which includes knowledge, belief, art, morals, law, custom and any other capabilities and habits acquired by man as a member of society." This definition emphasizes that culture is a social heritage and is the gift of society to mankind. However, anthropologists have made a distinction between 'culture' and 'civilization'. Culture is regarded as the moral, spiritual and intellectual attainments of man, whereas civilization is something outside us and consists of material culture, technology and social institutions. Civilization reveals the external properties and development of a society whereas the term 'culture' covers the entire field of man's achievements. Culture encompasses all forms of art, recreation and language. It is plural and its plurality includes ideas, languages, forms of worship, architecture, dress and handicrafts, which contribute to its continuity and richness. It means culture does not include only art, music, dance and drama but a whole way of life. In the words of Gurveen Kaur (2003: 5): "The word 'culture' is used in two different ways. One could be called the 'thin' notion of culture and the other the 'thick' notion of culture. The 'thin' notion refers to the style of dressing, cuisine, music, arts, dances and languages. The 'thick' notion is more comprehensive. It connotes a whole way of living—the integrated web of ideas, values, traditions, customs and habits that give a society/community its distinctive life-style." While the 'thin' notion of culture involves material (visible) components, the 'thick' notion of culture involves non-material (invisible) components. The former relates to physical objects like artifacts of the community but the latter to knowledge, beliefs, values, principles, ethics, and the whole way of human life. In the discourse of multiculturalism, it is the non-material components of culture that are always taken into consideration.

The term culture has attained larger dimensions of meaning over the years. One of the early scholars of cultural studies in Britain, Williams Raymond (1963: 16), defines culture as "an individual habit of mind; the state of intellectual development of a whole society; the arts; and the whole way of life of a group or people." The aim of culture is to pursue perfection in all walks of life. It is capable of developing the faculties of man in a harmonious and balanced manner. So the cultural man perfects not only himself but also the world. Williams Raymond challenges the Victorian practice of explaining culture as something that pertains to the upper and middle classes. Williams does not exclude any class, even the lower class, from the scope of culture. According to him, culture is a way of life which has its bearings not only on art and learning but also on institutions and ordinary behaviour. He argues that culture is a process of training, not merely a body of intellectual and imaginative work. With the passage of time, culture gained newer dimensions with respect to social, economic and political changes.

The 19th century British poet-critic, Mathew Arnold (1966: 48-49), has defined culture in various ways. According to him: "It is sweetness and light, it is the best that has been thought and said, it is internal to the human mind and general to the whole community; it is a harmony of all the powers that make for the beauty and worth of human nature." These definitions underline culture's dynamism and its presence in every aspect of social life. The individual who internalizes culture, Arnold says, has the qualities of a real human being. In T.S. Eliot's (1962: 120) opinion: "Culture means the way of life of a particular people living together in one place. That culture is made visible in their arts, in their social system, in their habits and customs and in their religion."

However, each culture has its own distinctive flavour and characteristics, even in the individual representing that culture. The values, pleasures, pains and gestures of an individual bear the imprint of his culture. Culture has its own regulatory force which enables it to approve/disapprove of certain forms of behaviour and way of life. It can thus control the nature of human relations and stabilizes them. As Abidi Hussain (1978: 3) says: "Culture is a sense of ultimate value possessed by a particular society as expressed in its collective institutions, by its individual members in their depositions, feelings, attitudes and manners as well as in significant forms which they give to material objects."

Culture can be imbibed directly from our social contacts and indirectly from television, movies, books, magazines, etc. Since it is basic to the defining of individuals and society, its role in preserving the character of human race is great. Thus, according to Laudin Harvey (1973: 84): "Culture is for man what water is for fish and air is for birds." And Edward Said (1994: 262) has something more enlightening to say about culture: "Culture is never just a matter of ownership, of borrowing and lending with absolute debtors and creditors, but rather of appropriations, common experiences, and interdependencies of all kinds among different cultures." He also underlines the influence of culture on arts, literature, communication, etc.

Literature and Culture

Culture and literature are mutually related. Literature is more than a realistic depiction of human life. It highlights the whole panorama of human life by subsuming in it the cultural traits, institutions, social stratifications and power structures of a society. Thus, literature enshrines in it all the cultural aspects of a society including its beliefs, knowledge, values and practices. Edward Said (1991: 27) has acknowledged the interrelationship between literature, culture and society thus: "Too often literature and culture are presumed to be politically, even historically innocent; it has regularly seemed otherwise to me, and certainly my study of Orientalism has convinced me that society and culture can only be understood and studied together."

Further, literature embodies social, cultural and universal values which can affect human life in various ways. A literary work is organic, holding within it a number of cultural themes. As Terry Eagleton (1996: 17) says: "Literary work itself comes to be seen as a mysterious organic unity, in contrast to the fragmented individualism of the capitalist marketplace: it is 'spontaneous' rather than rationally calculated, creative, rather than mechanical."

Literary creation has its roots in various social spheres such as language, economics, politics, race, ethnicity, class, gender and culture. A text thus is an organic unity of socio-cultural relations, racial differences, religious ideologies, class conflicts, gender biases, etc. Through it one can view the web of human relations and values of a society. The study of literature of a country, therefore, can be enlightening. African literature, for instance, puts before the international audience of various cultural aspects pertaining to Africa. It is through the means of literature that the international audience becomes aware of the 'life' of various countries. Indeed history and the press can keep people informed of other cultures, but literature takes them closer to human life and hence it is more appealing. Thus, isolating culture from literature is impossible as literature depicts human life that is deeply embedded in a particular culture.

Of all forms of literature, the novel has greater scope in critiquing human life and social culture. The canvas of the novelist is vast and as a social being he can depict, at any length, the changing relations of life in their social and cultural contexts and transform them into art. It may, therefore, be said that the success of the novelist depends on the intensity with which he depicts the cultural roots of the society he presents in his work. In general, literature shapes and changes social thinking and makes its audience more sensitive to his/others' position in social culture.

Multiculturalism: A Sociological Approach

The term multiculturalism was primarily used in the U.S.A. in connection with the demand of the black and other minority communities for equal representation in American society, including schools and colleges. Over the years, multiculturalism has gained the status of a movement. It insists that American society has never been 'white' but has been multi-racial having diverse backgrounds. As a movement, multiculturalism seeks to underscore the value of distinctly different ethnic, racial and cultural communities which cannot be allowed to melt into a common culture. It subsumes within it a lot of human differences which primarily include race, ethnicity, culture, religion, national origin, occupation, socio-economic status, age and gender. The scope of multiculturalism is very vast. As a social theory, it is relevant to all people representing various backgrounds. At the same time it can also be a framework which can be used as standard for evaluating one's values, beliefs and perceptions about cultural diversity, human rights and privileges in a society.

Like other '-isms', multiculturalism also has different connotations and implications, both positive and negative. Multiculturalism is not a body of homogeneous ideas. Rather it is a body of different ideas and opinions. Multicultural societies vary in their composition and, consequently, there are different versions of multiculturalism. Definitions of multiculturalism will illustrate this point. According to Turner Terence (1994: 419): "Multiculturalism is one manifestation of the postmodernist reaction to the delegitimization of the state and the erosion of the hegemony of the dominant culture in advanced capitalist countries." Postmodernism celebrates the rights of all classes and castes. Thus, it upholds the rights of women, African-Americans, dalits, homosexuals, etc. It also makes use of the culture, religion, knowledge and belief of the non-West for defining human rights. As Ziauddin Sarkar (2005: 236) says: "Postmodernism seeks to give voice to all cultures, decentres the 'centre' while making the 'periphery' the center of all cultural action and gives 'voice' to the 'voiceless', it is projected as a new and great force of liberation."

Multiculturalism also draws ideas from postcolonial theory which stands for the rights of the marginalized and weaker sections of society. As Leela Gandhi (1998: 42) says: "Post colonialism has found itself in the company of disciplines such as women's studies, cultural studies and gay/lesbian studies." It aims to challenge the center while being in the periphery. Andrew Milner has talked about the relationship between postcolonialism and multiculturalism. He argues that both the theories have invoked a discourse of difference. Edward Said, one of the earliest postcolonial theorists, has critiqued the Western/European attitude of superiority and the Europeans' prejudice against the non-Western cultures, especially African and Indian cultures. They classify Eastern cultures as Oriental cultures or 'others'. European histories projected the Easterners culturally backward, sensual and passive. According to Said, Western histories have only projected Oriental culture as something inferior and worthless. Said's idea of orientalism underscores the basic point that the West's ideas of the East were meant to create discriminations and imposing power structures. The ideas often reinforced the hegemony of the West. Edward Said (1985: 7) has explained the term 'hegemony' in Gramscian terms: "In any society not totalitarian, then, certain cultural forms predominate over others, just as certain ideas are more influential than others; the form of this cultural leadership is what Gramsci has identified as hegemony, an indispensable concept for any understanding of cultural life in the industrial West. It is hegemony, or rather the result of cultural hegemony at work, that gives Orientalism the durability and the strength."

Multiculturalism does not exist merely as a subject of debate and discussion. It has been adopted in the policy decisions made in countries like Canada, Australia and U.K. As an official policy, multiculturalism succeeds to create socio-cultural harmony, mutual tolerance and respect among different cultures. It not only recognizes the fact of cultural diversity but also holds that such differences should be respected and publicly affirmed. It is a process of appreciating cultural diversity and enabling the visible minorities to attain equality and social justice. It also encourages different ethnic groups to preserve their ethno-cultural identity and sustain their religious and cultural beliefs, rituals, customs, traditions and their lifestyles comprising food habits, dress codes and different socio-cultural practices.

The bearing of multiculturalism on other areas of knowledge has been acknowledged by many. In the opinion of Judith Squires (2002: 114): "Multiculturalism has become the topic of the moment, not only for political theorists, but also for social theorist, Sociologists, political scientists and educationalists." Because of its relation to various disciplines, it has derived various themes from them. These are:

M

U ➔ Harmonious co-existence of multiple cultures and subcultures.

L ➔ Value of tolerance.

T ➔ Equal respect and value to all cultures (non-discrimination).

I ➔ Privileges and protection to minority cultures.

C ➔ Diversity: Cultural, religious, ethnic.

U ➔ Cultural liberty.

L ➔ Identity: cultural, community, ethnic, religious.

T ➔ Recognition: minority cultures, recognition of differences.

U ➔ Equality: cultural groups, equal opportunity.

R ➔ Socio-cultural harmony.

A ➔ Special rights, privileges and exemptions for minority cultures.

L ➔ Social heterogeneity and diversity.

I ➔ A movement for social change.

S ➔ Opposition to cultural imperialism.

M

Multiculturalism acknowledges the presence of many cultures and as a value it legitimizes the relevance of all of them in a geo-political area. It acknowledges cultural pluralism based on race, ethnicity and language. Alex Thio (1997: 44) argues: "The coexistence of numerous subcultures can develop into multiculturalism, a state in which all subcultures are equal to one another in the same society." The harmonious co-existence of diverse culture is a sign of a healthy society. Such a society is characterized by co-operation, tolerance, forbearance, respect and understanding of each cultural group. Multiculturalism establishes cultural contacts, exchanges cultural ideologies and promotes the values of 'harmonious co-existence' of many cultures—dominant, superordinate, subordinate, minority, weak, marginal, patriarchal, etc. As an '-ism', it endorses the idea of difference and heterogeneity that is exemplified in the concept of diversity. It does not simply point to the presence of many cultures within the nation-state but admits 'distinctiveness' and 'uniqueness' of each culture, which makes human life more varied and meaningful. Each of the many cultures, present in a society, is unique and heterogeneous entity. So 'distinctiveness' and 'uniqueness' of each culture needs to be recognized and considered separately.

Tolerance is a recent political term used in social, cultural and religious debates. It vigorously contradicts discrimination. It is an affirmative value of multiculturalism, which enhances the strength of a multicultural society. A commonly held view suggests that being multicultural involves tolerance towards racial, cultural and religious differences. In a multicultural society, race, culture and religion all foster their own set of values and rules. If we tolerate racial differences, cultural plurality and religious diversity, it helps to minimize the chances of conflict and friction in society. As Ramakant Sinari (2002: 20) says: "From a utilitarian point of view tolerance on the part of everybody is a prerequisite for the world community's unity, stability and progress, it ought to be the norm of one's behaviour irrespective of the nature of circumstances one happens to be in." Tolerance is a positive force, which facilitates good relations in human society. In a vibrant multicultural society, we need to tolerate and respect differences, may be cultural, religious or racial. But difference should not be treated as a deficiency of a specific culture or a group. Therefore, tolerance needs to be considered as a positive value of multiculturalism, which seeks social harmony, peace and coexistence.

Multiculturalism ensures equal respect and value to all cultures. In a sense, each culture contains something that is valuable and admirable. Therefore, all cultures deserve equal respect and value. In this regard Sarah Joseph (2002: 159) views: "Multiculturalism is used to refer to a desired end-state, as a way of referring to a society in which different cultures are respected and the reproduction of culturally defined group is protected and social diversity celebrated." Each culture gives stability, strength and meaning to human life and holds its members together as a community. It is obvious that respect for culture means respect for a community's right. So culture offers us the overall quality and value of a good life. Respecting culture entails respect to community, principles, beliefs, thoughts, practices and lifestyles. Different cultures represent and characterize different systems of meaning and vision of a good life. Therefore, multiculturalism responds to the issue of cultural discrimination by privileging the goal of respecting minority cultures.

Blum Lawrence (1998: 89) says: "It is the task of educators to teach multiculturalism in a way that shows the kind of respect for cultures that is appropriate to them and does not push toward a meaningless comparison between different cultures in terms of their overall value." It means there is no point of comparing one culture with another, because all cultures are equally rich and deserve equal value and respect. And there is no objective evidence for claiming that some cultures are 'inferior' or 'superior' for human development and social stability. Bhikhu Parekh (2002:136) remarks on the equal value of culture:

> Multiculturalism makes culture the central fact of moral and political life and is committed to some form of moral relativism. It holds that individuals are culturally embedded and shaped, that their culture is the most important fact of their life, that cultures are self-contained wholes and neither permit nor can be evaluated by transcultural and universal standards, that they are or should be presumed to be equal value, and that cultural practices need no further authority than the fact they are part of a group's culture.

Advocates of multiculturalism view that all cultures, especially minority cultures within a society, should be protected and made secure. The idea of preserving cultures is a way of recognizing minority cultures and representing them as equals in the pubic arena. Multiculturalism values dignity and status of the minority cultures. Irrespective of colour, caste, origin and nationality, all the minority cultures should be protected and respected. This kind of humanitarian approach enhances social integrity and peace. Gurpreet Mahajan (2002: 64) says: "Awareness about the dangers of cultural majoritarianism, coupled with the emphasis on cultural diversity, has made preservation of minority cultures a primary concern of multiculturalism." The preservation of minority cultures leads towards the creation of a healthy and strong human society. Today, almost every society is internally plural. If our democratic setup is to remain intact, we need to preserve and value all the minority cultures with their differences and uniqueness. Failing to do this can engender endless ethnic violence and confrontations. Therefore, one of the primary concerns of multiculturalism is the minimizing of cultural discrimination and respecting minority cultures. As a result, the liberal capitalist societies in the West have accepted the policy of promoting tolerance and respect for minority cultures. These societies have recognized multiculturalism as a social theory, one of the means of constructing a stable human society.

Multiculturalism is a new coinage with different implications. Its close relation to the postcolonial nations is well known. John Rex (1996: 136) says: "Diversity has to be recognized within ethnic communities, as well as between the separate communities, and there must be the possibility of political expression for a variety of different types of individuals with differing types of affiliation to their own communities. The notion of diversity receives a positive value in the discourse of multiculturalism." It suggests that each culture has an individualized particularity, and that uniqueness should be appreciated. Canada, one of the multicultural nations, has adopted multiculturalism as an official policy and successfully manages its increasing diversity and multiplicity. By providing equal rights and balancing common responsibilities to all the citizens, Canada attempts to cherish multiculturalism. Their endorsing diversity has taught them to accept and respect diverse views. Therefore, the presence of diverse cultures enhances our self-awareness and offers alternative ways of life.

Multiculturalism values cultural diversity as it enriches our lives and widens our horizons. If we recognise the richness of cultural diversity of the world, we can easily minimize the severity of some problems like social conflicts, discrimination, racism, xenophobia, caste and gender related intolerance. Cultural diversity does not merely include the visible products, like food, clothes and style, but it implies freedom to the people in a pluralistic society. Gurpreet Mahajan (2002: 146) says: "Multiculturalism is not just a statement on the discrimination of cultural minorities in the nation-state; it represents an agenda in which promoting cultural diversity is considered an essential condition for ensuring equal treatment for all communities within the polity." It means cultural diversity encourages a healthy competition between different systems of ideas and ways of life. After all, culture does not exist in a vacuum, but exists in different social groups. So cultural diversity becomes an integral part of human existence, and affiliating oneself to it is essential for a peaceful life. Cultural diversity is valuable, because it teaches one to identify oneself with others or compares oneself with others. Diversity also opens up the possibility of having dialogues with varied ethnic groups and thus evaluates various parties, involved in the dialogues, their socio-cultural identities.

Religious diversity can be explored from psychological, anthropological, sociological and historical perspectives. Tolerating another religion might not be a great task. But engaging oneself in the religious ideologies of various religions and acknowledging and appreciating them are essential features of true multiculturalism. Only such healthy exchanges can bring about peace in a multireligious society, which is a common entity across the world. The culture of a country is often shaped by its religions as well. Therefore, the people who have imbibed the culture have in them the elements of all these religions. So it may be hard to say that one religion is bad while other is good. Multiculturalism highlights this aspect.

Like religious diversity, ethnic diversity is also a characteristic feature of any multicultural society. Ethnic diversity has often led to rivalries and clashes. Each ethnic group, multiculturalism implies, has its own value system that is dear to it. A minority's cultural heritage cannot easily be shattered by a majority culture, although such shattering has already taken place in the world. The important fact is that ethnic diversity opposes ethnocentrism and promotes regular interaction between minority and majority cultures.

Human life and its development depend considerably on cultural liberty. Although tradition has its value, individual cultures progress by expanding their liberty for making their own choices. The Human Development Report (2004: 13) has underlined the importance of cultural liberty: "Cultural liberty is an important aspect of human freedom, central to the capability of people to live as they would like and to have the opportunity to choose from the options they have—or can have." Cultural liberty lends newer dimensions to values, beliefs and various social practices and it can expand so without harming the multicultural fabric of a society. Multicultural democracies prosper with the prosperity of cultural liberty.

Indeed multiculturalism involves identity politics but it is a politics of difference. According to Lucius Outlaw (1998: 391): "One of the complex forms of the 'politics of difference' appears in struggles over 'multiculturalism' as a replacement for hegemonic monoculturalism." One advantage of multiculturalism, as has already mentioned, is that it challenges the hegemony of a single dominant culture and attempts to strengthen the ties between other cultural groups by appropriating their differences. The upper hand of one culture is thus discouraged. Thus, multiculturalism has many beneficial functions: it prioritizes cultural pluralism; encourages social heterogeneity; and it sensitizes societies to the dangers of cultural dominance, hegemony and governance. The politics of difference points to the fact that any modern multicultural society ought to acknowledge its cultural diversity and identity related differences. As Rajeev Bhargava (2002: 100) points out: "Multiculturalism brings together a number of distinct themes such as identity, recognition, cultural belonging, which all respond to common human needs but are understood and dealt with variously in different societies."

The common sociological assumption about 'identity' is that it mostly pertains to the individual. But the postmodern era has lent its wider connotations. Identity no longer has a monolithic implication but it now carries the notion of multiple identities, which include culture, group, ethnicity, religion, community, nation and universal identity. Such implications constitute identity politics. The individual of the present times, when s/he moves around the borderless world, carries with him all these implications of his identity and apparently the postmodern world has begun to acknowledge them.

Samuel Freeman (2002: 19) argues: "Multiculturalists advocate that one's cultural identity is so central to a person's good, each distinct cultural group in a multicultural society should recognize and respect the cultural practices of others and not impose its norms, particularly its liberal norms, on them." Cultural identity pertains to an individual's affinity to his/her own particular cultural group which shares certain values and bonds. It also involves the visible as well as invisible aspects of a specific culture that differentiates its people from those of other cultures.

Community identity also forms a major issue in multicultural studies. Surinder Jodhka (2002: 296) says: "Multiculturalism came to be viewed as a possible way of dealing with the problem of equality among groups and communities. As a framework of state policy it recognized cultural differences and community identities as politically significant realities and advocated for their participation in the functioning of political processes as collective agents." Multiculturalists are of the opinion that in a non-homogeneous nation-state minority communities can be at a disadvantageous position. Majority communities in a nation-state can maintain social advantageous positions which can lead to the prejudiced marginalization of 'lesser' communities. And the marginalization can deprive them of their rights and opportunities. The agenda of multiculturalism consists of strategies which can resist such deprivations. So that the less privileged also get the opportunity to extend their relations with the wider society. Thus, the value of community identity and its distinctiveness are respected. Further, each community is encouraged to explore their potentialities in a society providing equal opportunities. Again, multiculturalism's community identity stands above all kinds of elimination and humiliation of the marginalized groups.

Another aspect that forms a major theme of multiculturalism is ethnic identity. Dusan D. (1994: 111) explains: "Multiculturalism is a human, democratic and civilized act of the society applying it, with a declared position and supporting legislation that members of different ethnic communities should be allowed to express their own cultural/ethnic identity freely." The ethnic identity of an individual is a part of his consciousness. The terms 'minority' and 'ethnic' are sometimes used synonymously in order to identify groups which share a common language, race, relation or nationality. However, with the surprising progress in the means of transport and availability of jobs, Western countries have acknowledged the necessity of being multi-religious and multi-ethnic. Ethnic identity helps one to distinguish oneself from the other groups of a society. Ethnicity puts the respective groups under a single umbrella with its different colors of language, religion, race, nationality and common cultural markers.

Religious identity is a powerful theme in democratic and secular politics. However, over-consciousness of one's religion can lead to clashes with other religions. Indeed globalization has accelerated migration and the flow of people from one country to another. The consequence of such movement is religious assortment at a global level. Yet there are occasions when religions clash. The purpose of multiculturalism is to avoid such religious frictions in a society and create the awareness that helps to keep each religion's religiosity intact. However, it is also a fact that religion is often politicized especially when it comes to the sharing of political power. Politicization of religion often leads to the loss of its ideological face. Multiculturalism treats religion as a spiritual force which can stabilize human life and, as such, asserts that religious identities should be protected and respected.

In the discourse of multiculturalism, the concept of recognition occupies an important position. The concept of recognition includes the recognition of differences and equality. Charles Taylor (1994: 25) explains recognition of differences thus: "Nonrecognition or misrecognition...can be a form of oppression, imprisoning someone in a false, distorted, reduced mode of being. Beyond simple lack of respect, it can inflict a grievous wound, saddling people with crippling self-hatred.

Due recognition is not just a courtesy, but a vital human need." The reason why multiculturalism highlights recognition is to remove social marginalization, dispossession and exclusion of minority cultures. These cultures, in the present times, tend to demand the recognition of their distinctiveness and equality in polity. They argue that their differences must be appreciated at the societal level and there should be equal and fair treatment to all. Will Kymlicka (1997: 10) says: "Modern societies are increasingly confronted with minority groups demanding recognition of their identity, and accommodation of their cultural differences." A multicultural society is a learning society. The various cultures and groups learn new things through healthy interactions and appropriate them for their own advancement. Multiculturalism pulls down barriers of discrimination and exclusion.

Among the different forms of recognition, the recognition of minority culture has received the special attention of multiculturalists. Their attempt is to bring to the notice of the wider public the deprivation of minority cultures. They attempt to highlight the struggle of these cultures due to non-recognition. They stand for the equalization of different cultures and communities which can contribute to social harmony and peace. Gurpreet Mahajan (2002: 11) remarks: "Multiculturalism is concerned with the issue of equality: it asks whether the different communities, living peacefully together, co-exist as equals in the public arena." Every culture has its own limitation and only dialogue between disparate cultures can sort out the issues of difference. Such dialogues can be very fruitful when the participants in them have openness of mind and the willingness to acknowledge other's points of view.

The idea of equal opportunity that multiculturalism advocates has cultural sensitivity. C.R. Steven (1994: 88) argues: "All human beings as the bearers of a universal human nature—as persons—are of equal value from the democratic perspective, and all people as persons deserve equal respect and equal opportunity for self-realization. The principle of equal opportunity supports both majority and minorities for enjoying their cultures equally." The success of equal opportunity depends on its practice in the actual socio-cultural and political contexts rather on its theorization.

Socio-cultural harmony is a matter of great importance in any multicultural society. The health of such a society can be ensured when it grows beyond inter-ethnic, inter-racial discriminations and cultural jealousies. Here, too, multiculturalists underline the necessity of dialogues. As Valierian Rodrigues (2002: 126) rightly points out: "Multiculturalism is an invitation to dialogue. Given our largely culture and community bound social existence; our knowledge and understanding remain necessarily limited. Such a limitation can be transcended only by getting into an active dialogue with other communities and identities. In the process of this dialogue other communities may arise, including those who bear multiple and over laden identities." Dialogues pave the way for the intimacy of diverse groups and their harmonious existence.

The minority cultures have more deprivations; therefore, multiculturalism upholds the idea of granting special privileges for and exemptions to them. The privileges pertain to religious practices, mode of worship, invitation ceremonies, dress codes, food habits, etc. In Western democracies, minorities of other countries have been granted special concessions and privileges. The example of Sikhs in Canada and Britain is a case in point. They are exempted from wearing helmets while riding motorcycles. The Sikhs, a minority culture in these countries, enjoy an exemption which has associations with their religious dress code. Even in India, the constitution ensures protection to religious practices of all communities and grants minorities special rights to preserve their language and culture.

In the postcolonial situation, differences in terms of wealth, talent, status, interest and opinion matter a lot. Multiculturalism has its roots in the politics of diversity and heterogeneity. As such promoting heterogeneity and diversity are two of its basic concerns. The purpose of such promotion is the generation of cultural hybridity and novelty, which bring variety in human life.

The importance of multiculturalism as a social movement is being recognized. The focus of it as a movement is to protect the marginalized groups against impositions of the dominant groups. As C. Upadhya (2002: 187) summarizes Terence Turner's views on multiculturalism: "He believes that criticism of the use of the term 'culture' in multiculturalism discourse are off the mark, because multiculturalism is not an intellectual discipline but a movement for social change. It is a mode of struggle by oppressed and marginalized groups against the cultural hegemony of dominant ethnic groups." As a movement multiculturalism aims at the empowerment of the weaker sections of society.

All forms of cultural imperialism and homogenization are an anathema to multiculturalism. What it admires is the originality and identity of distinct cultures. Imposition of values, systems or styles by a dominant culture is never welcome. Underlining these facts, Rajeev Bhargava (1999: 19) says: "Multiculturalism opposes cultural imperialism and homogenization." Multiculturalists are aware of the emergence of cultural imperialism of the recent times and they oppose it by arguing for cultural conservatism.

All "-isms" have invited different interpretations and multiculturalism is no exception. Social scientists and political interpreters have defined multiculturalism in their own ways and, as such, they have added new dimensions to its meaning. Needless to say, these meanings are sometimes contradictory and ambiguous. Some treat it as a divisive phenomenon which can give birth to a new racism in the world. It breaks the homogeneity of human societies and brings in disintegration and unrest at national and international level. Its eulogization of multiple identities and cultural traditions can be a threat to democracy. The complaint of the conservative opponents is that multiculturalism confines itself to a few minority groups which are socially underprivileged and marginalized. They fear that such confinement can endanger national unity and stability. And the anthropologists have their own reservations. They argue that multiculturalism violates and vulgarizes their key ideas of cultural relativism by essentializing cultural differences. They feel that multiculturalism is more superficial and philosophical than practical. A contemporary anti-multiculturalist, Brian Barry has critiqued some of the basic assumptions of multiculturalists. Bikhu Parekh (1994: 137) has summarized Brian Barry's criticism thus: "For Barry, multiculturalism is a muddled, incoherent and pernicious doctrine it is relativist, anti-egalitarian, illiberal, morally conservative, socially divisive and subversive of politically community. It denies common standards for evaluating cultures and yet insists that all cultures are or should be presumed to be equal value...it ignores serious forms of injustice and inequality and is the enemy of progresses." Thus, it becomes clear that despite the popularity of multiculturalism in the recent years, it has invited adverse comments which essentially challenge its basic assumptions.

Forms of Multiculturalism

Movements based on theoretical assumptions can give rise to different currents within themselves. These currents of thought, while widening the scope of a movement, can also give shape to independent forms the same movement. Multiculturalism, too, has different forms. The major forms are discussed briefly in the following lines.

Democratic Multiculturalism recognizes the reality of cultural diversity and differences and gives them a political dimension. These differences can give rise to clashes between groups but democratic multiculturalism attempts to resolve conflicts through dialogue and discussion. It assumes that social equality is possible only when there is no oppression and subordination. The focal themes of democratic multiculturalism are social heterogeneity, diversity and freedom. It advocates the politics of involvement. Another kind is conservative multiculturalism which is less accommodative than the other forms. Liberal multiculturalism celebrates the value of individualism. Liberty and autonomy are terms dear to it, but it denies the issues of identity and belonging. Its argument is for a natural equality of all—Whites, African-Americans and Asians. Intellectual sameness of races is an idea that this form of multiculturalism has always upheld. It endorses universalism, adopts the principle of equality among the races and communities and celebrates diversity, but only at the individual level. Critical multiculturalism focuses itself on the importance of the positive socio-cultural transformations. It supports the representations of race, class and gender in the public domain and understands the reasons of social unrest and struggles. The important themes in corporate multiculturalism are the possibilities of global market, based on the transportation of knowledge and elaborate international comparativism. It envisages a borderless free world based on new knowledge, global capital and global marketing. Polycentric multiculturalism has its bearing on art and art forms like music, film and other cultural goods. It also highlights the value of multiple identities and heterogeneity. Insurgent multiculturalism is educational in the sense that it advocates changes in curricula. It values the teacher-taught relationship and encourages teachers and students to cross boundaries to attain knowledge, which is the capital of the postmodern period.

Multiculturalism in India

Here we discuss Indian multiculturalism in detail as we have chosen Indian novels in English for multicultural analysis. Multiculturalism is a multifaceted and flexible social theory that keeps India integrated, though the country's social fabric is complex and intricate. For knowing Indian multiculturalism, it is essential to know the social, cultural and religious history of India. Indian society is composed of people belonging to a variety of religions, sects, castes and tribes. The history of transformation from Vedic religion to Hindu religion is a long and complex one. The growth of caste, patriarchal practices and religious movements has occupied an important place in shaping Indian society in relation to national integration/ disintegration and homogeneity/heterogeneity at all levels. Hinduism, a powerful religion, has a caste system in which one's superior or inferior status is determined by birth. The dominance of Brahmans in the hierarchies of caste, gender and culture had been very powerful in pre-independent India. But apart from caste and religion, there have been a variety of factors that have divided people. After independence, we found a number of disintegrating factors beginning to demand their rights and cry for recognition. It is obvious that the basis of Hinduism is the caste system, which is specially geared to preserve and promote 'upper' caste hegemony that is based on the systematic exploitation and oppression of the so-called 'lower' and 'subordinate' classes. At present, Hindutava represents the contemporary agenda of Brahmanism. It poses an immense threat not just to the Muslims of the country, but also to the vast majority of the so-called 'Dalit-Bahujans'. It is often believed that Hindutava preserves and promotes 'upper' caste rule and 'lower' caste slavery. It means Indian history speaks a lot about Hindutavawadis, who have been reluctant to work for the welfare and benefit of Dalits, Muslims, Christians and the Adivasi tribes. On the contrary, they have supported and entertained the capitalist-Brahminical elites.

Looking at the social history of India, it is argued that the downfall of Buddhism gave rise to Brahmanism. According to Dr. Babasaheb Ambedkar, the architect of Indian constitution, Brahmanism brought a number of (negative) changes. It made the Brahmans a class of privileged people; it brought about conflicts and anti-social feelings between different castes and changed things for making them suitable for their interest. Dr. Ambedkar, also a leading revolutionary of Dalit-Bahujan movement, insisted that the true religion should be rationalist, based on truth. Even Mahatma Gandhi, the father of our nation, was always struggling for the emancipation of untouchables. He wanted to develop a sense of unity among all the people, irrespective of their castes, communities, groups and gender. His chief aim was to improve the miserable condition of the untouchables and the deprived classes belonging to the various sections of society. As a nationalist, he devoted his life to Indian masses and tried to keep homogeneity between Hindus and Muslims. However, the non-Brahman leaders of the social reform movement started attacking Brahmanism and adopted the action programme of breaking several rules of caste and gender. Among all those social reformers, Mahatma Phule was a revolutionary thinker who promoted non-Brahman thinking in the modern period. According to Phule, Brahmanism is a powerful system of oppression to women, peasants and untouchables. Therefore, he reacted against the ordination of caste and the performance of rituals by the Brahman priests. He offered Sarvajanik Satyadharma, i.e. universal religion of truth and proclaimed equality among men, women, peasants and untouchables. As a social thinker, Phule tried to solve many socio-economic problems by imparting education, especially to the women and untouchables. Chhatrapati Shahu Maharaj was also one of the social revolutionaries who struggled against Brahman bureaucracy. He fought against the domination and supremacy of Brahmans in education, administration and politics. He was an early originator and a designer of the reservation policy for backward and underprivileged classes. As a revolutionary social reformer, he made primary education compulsory, especially to the girls and less privileged classes in society. Apart from the above mentioned social reformers and activists, there were others like Raja Ram Mohan Roy, M.G. Ranade and Maharshi Karve who had taken up social issues such as the abolition of 'sati' and remarriage of the widows.

However, the notion of identity seems to be one of the important aspects of Indian multiculturalism. Identity involves a sense of belongingness of people to country, caste, class, religion, etc. Identity also relates to the culture and language which a group represents. India in the past was known as Vedic India, Buddhist India, Hindu India and today we call it secular India. It shows that the identity of India was/is known by the religion, culture and language of her people. In fact, the issue of identity is not important to those who belong to the dominant culture/religion/society, but it is important to those who are 'broken' 'marginalized' and 'outsiders'. For Hindus, caste is one of the important marks of identification. Each caste group has its distinct identity and diverse ways of life. Since the members of several castes were called Hindus, they were supposed to uniformly worship Hindu gods and goddesses in temple, but some of them were not allowed to enjoy their religious and civil rights. Especially, the earlier inhabitants like Adivasi communities and untouchables were disadvantaged and deprived of their religious practices and civil rights. Even, today, many of the Adivasi communities are deprived of their rights and are dislocated and dislodged due to some dominant forces.

Besides religion and caste as categories of grouping in Indian society, gender is also an important category. In Vedic period, women were not allowed to recite or listen to Vedic hymns and were treated as subordinate and inferior. In the words of S.M. Dahiwale (2005: 12): "In traditional Hindu order, a woman is not viewed to be independent, because she is protected in her childhood by her parents, after marriage by her husband and in the old age by her son." This clearly shows how Indian patriarchy is quite rude and old in controlling the 'second sex'. But in the postmodern period, the status of Indian woman has changed and the compartmentalization between men and women is being broken down.

Yes, disparities and discripancies exist in Indian society. So the anti-Brahmin movement is considered to be a source of elimination of social inequality and discrimination between castes and communities, which have been always oppressed for centuries. This movement has even initiated a progamme against religion, gender and caste discrimination and prejudice. In short, anti-Brahman movement attempts to maintain the unity and harmony of the oppressed, untouchables, adivasis, Muslims, Christians and other underprivileged minority groups.

Taking into account the postmodern scenario of Indian multiculturalism, we notice a number of changes and transformations. In the postmodern period, there is no country in the world where one can find an ethnically, racially and culturally homogeneous population. Due to globalization and modernization, the world has become a global village. As we know, India is a multicultural society, which is dissected on the basis of religion, caste and class. But the boundaries of such groups have always been overlapping. At present, people from different religions and communities have started respecting and tolerating each other's religious faith and cultural practices. As

Rasheeduddin Khan (1987: 35) says: "India has been one of the greatest confluences of cultural strands, a laboratory of racial intermixing, of cross-fertilization of religious ideas and secular thought, of coexistence of language and dialects, a veritable microcosm of the globe." It means people belonging to different religions and communities are intermixed with each other without discarding their own habits, customs and modes of living. It is a fact that India's culture is deeply rooted in an age-old ethos. It is a fascinating country, because of its diversity and multiplicity of languages, varieties of gods and goddesses, values and beliefs, customs and practices. From the very beginning, diversity has been a fundamental characteristic of India. India has managed its increasing diversity and maintained unity by balancing individual and collective rights in its constitution. India's anti-colonial, nationalist leaders had taken the right step to promote her multicultural reality. Among the nationalist leaders, the first prime minister of India, Pandit Nehru, had recognized India's diversity and emphasized the concept of 'unity in diversity'. In his words (1946: 61-62): "The diversity of India is tremendous; it is obvious. It lies on the surface and anybody can see it. It concerns itself with physical appearances as well as with certain mental habits and traits.... Yet, with all these differences, there is no mistaking the impress of India." India as a multicultural polity has adopted the institutional form of constitutionalism that appropriately promotes and encourages the concept of 'unity in diversity'. In this regard R. Sudarshan (1999: 101) rightly says:

> Unity in diversity, an oft-repeated aspiration in India, seeks to accommodate differences within a framework of shared basic values and common interests. Such a framework requires the conviction that unity is best fostered by tolerating diversity, that dissenting views should freely coexist with the dominant values of society, and interaction among diverse peoples, ethnic and religious groups, cultures and sub-cultures is a positive force for creativity, innovation and change.

Perhaps, India was among the first major democracies in the world to recognize and respect diverse cultures, communities, religions and languages. This suggests a significant and creditable initiative on the part of democratic India's early political leadership. Indian constitution has recognized diversity and it values equal citizenship and equal rights. The constitutional form of pluralism guarantees inclusion and provides autonomy to all castes and communities for their cultural and religious practices. Due to sufficient amount of freedom, religious minorities, with few exceptions, have enjoyed a reasonable degree of autonomy and liberty. The Constitution of India has also provided special rights for scheduled castes and scheduled tribes in the matters of employment and special quotas for admissions in educational institutions. The freedom is given to the minorities for observing and preserving their language, culture and religious practices and permitted them to establish and administer educational institutions of their choice. It means, India, a multicultural society, has adopted the institutional forms of constitutionalism, which is very close to the theory of multiculturalism. Therefore, it is said that Indian constitution is one of the most authentic documents of Indian multiculturalism. This policy framework of Indian Government helps the minority groups to safeguard their religion and culture. However, India officially celebrates 5 of Hindu holidays, 4 of Muslims, 2 of Christians, 1 of Buddhists, 1 of Jains and 1 of Sikhs in recognition of a diverse population (Human Development Report: 2004). This speaks a lot about India's multicultural reality.

The richness and plurality of Indian culture have received worldwide acclaim only because of its diversity and distinctiveness. Indian constitution has respected, promoted and valued all cultural groups equally. Nowadays, there is no feeling of threat, because of equal constitutional recognition of all religions, castes and ethnic groups. In connection with this, B.P. Singh (1999: 67) says: "No religion or group should have the feeling of a threat of being swamped. There are no 'majority' and 'minority' cultures. The smallest unit has its contribution to make to the enrichment of the national sum total, and must be respected." B.P. Singh's remark underscores the importance of Indian multiculturalism that appreciates cultural and religious diversity and enables the visible minorities to attain equity and social justice. It encourages different ethnic groups to preserve their ethno-cultural identities by sustaining their religious and cultural beliefs and values. The policy of multiculturalism in India expects social harmony and peaceful coexistence. It reflects cultural and racial diversity and acknowledges freedom to all members of society. In brief, Indian multiculturalism gives the messages, "live and let live", "unity in diversity", and "living together separately".

It is necessary to realize the actuality and authenticity of Indian multiculturalism in the postmodern period. Till now we have discussed different facets of Indian multiculturalism. But in the postmodern period, India's socio-political, religious and cultural face looks unusually strange. Although, there are provisions in the constitution for protecting minority rights, the suffering of the minorities has been a reality in India. There are some recent happenings in India, which create doubt and distrust about India's integration/disintegration. For instance, the brutish demolition of the Babri Masjid in Ayodhaya, bomb blasts in Mumbai, Godhra incident in Gujarat, communal riots in different parts of the country, violent disturbances, dislocation and the displacement of Adivasis. All instances show how these destabilizing factors in our country may influence and affect our national integration. Though we say India is a multicultural country, which has adopted a multicultural policy, it also poses some issues and faces some challenges because of the hidden casteism, communal politics, false secularism, criminalisation of politics, corruption, and many more issues related to language, culture and ethnicity. These issues still remain unresolved in India. After all, policies don't work only on a paper; it requires strong willpower to recognize and admit all the people with their distinctions and peculiarities. Here we make an attempt to expose the reality of Indian society. But in comparison with other multicultural countries, India's multicultural policy runs quite smoothly and efficiently. After all, any '-ism' has positive as well as negative implications, Indian multiculturalism is no exception. So Indian multicultural policy would be a sign of progress and not a disgrace.

Approach and Method of Study

In the postmodern period multiculturalism has acquired wider scope in the fields of politics, sociology, anthropology and literary studies. The arguments for and against were discussed and inspected in different contexts and perspectives by different social scientists and political thinkers, but there is no monistic outlook or view on multiculturalism. Due to its variety, multiculturalism has become an issue of debate, ambiguity and controversy. It has different dimensions and implications in different disciplines. Apart from its political and philosophical dimensions and implications, the present study makes an attempt to look at multiculturalism from sociological perspectives. In sociological writing, it is common to come across different perspectives, but the present study restricts with two perspectives. The first perspective is based on an integrative-adaptive model, which implies multiple ethno-cultural and religious identities, co-existing and constituting a cultural mosaic, whereas the second perspective is based on an ideology, constructed in order to legitimize the socio-economic inequalities between different ethnic groups. Here multiculturalism functions as a social ideology as well as a policy framework that allows socio-cultural distinctions and peculiarities. Each group within a mosaic has an equal right in sharing power. So, the concern of the present study is only with the above-mentioned perspectives on multiculturalism. However, in India, coexistence has not always been a reality and socio-economic inequalities between different ethnic groups can be seen in different sections of society. Therefore, in the present study, the discrepancies and inconsistencies reflected in the selected novels are subjected to critical investigation.

Multiculturalism is not a single doctrine, but is a body of different deliberations and principles. Therefore, the present study explores how different principles of multiculturalism are observed/violated in the selected novels, namely, Mulk Raj Anand's *Untouchable* (1935), Khushwant Singh's *Train to Pakistan* (1956), Anita Desai's *Bye Bye Blackbird* (1971) and Arundhati Roy's *The God of Small Things* (1997). India, being a multicultural country, has adopted and promoted multiculturalism as a social ideology as well as a policy framework. Taking into account this aspect, the present study analyses the selected novels from the sociological perspectives of multiculturalism.

The method of the present study involves a close and an indepth analysis of the selected novels. Selecting significant examples/extracts from the novels, an attempt has been made to analyze and examine these novels in the framework of multiculturalism. The present study is not only an attempt to perceive how different principles of multiculturalism are reflected in the novels, but also to examine how the violation of the principles of multiculturalism has led to social friction, conflict and disharmony. Therefore, there is the possibility of disparities and resemblances in the progression of analysis, because all the principles of multiculturalism are not uniformly and equally reflected or violated in the selected novels.

2

Multiculturalism in *Untouchable*

Mulk Raj Anand's *Untouchable* describes the experiences and thoughts of an eighteen-year old sweeper boy called Bakha, the protagonist of the novel. All the incidents of the novel take place on one single day, beginning at dawn and ending by nightfall. The story opens in the outcastes' colony where people from different low castes and communities live in very unhygienic conditions. The castes Hindus, on the other hand, live their comfortable and relaxed life in the village called Bulashah. The privileged caste Hindus cause mental depression to the untouchables and humiliate them in the name of purity and pollution. Bakha leads a hard life because of his extreme poverty, caste stigma and the kind of treatment he receives from the caste Hindus. He is a victim of the Indian caste system that has given birth to untouchability, a social evil. The whole story is based upon the caste Hindus' treatment of the untouchables, the deprived and oppressed classes. Throughout the day Bakha suffers a lot but remains mute, because of his caste stigma, poverty and oppressed existence. He tries to protest against the caste Hindus, but his inherited passivity makes him cool. As the protagonist, he is exposed to the influences of the modern world. But till the end he remains an inactive 'revolutionary' incapable of bringing about a personal revolution. *Untouchable* exposes valuable records of important phases in the history of Indian society where caste was a major hurdle in the progress of the untouchables.

The social structure of India is stratified with in-built inequalities and injustices based on the caste system. Although social stratification exists in almost all societies, the caste system is quite unique to the Indian society. Caste prejudices have existed in India, particularly among the Hindus, for a very long period of time. Of course, it has led to inequality and discrimination.

The Indian caste system is based on a Varna system, which divides people into four major divisions, namely, the Brahmins, the Kshatriyas, the Vaishyas and the Sudras. In addition to these four Varnas, there is a fifth group called the untouchables. They were considered as impure and polluted and were forced to undertake all menial jobs like sweeping, tanning, cleaning, etc. They were segregated, subjugated and harassed by the so-called 'pure' people. From the ancient period, the Varna system maintained a sharp social hierarchy. Though there were only four Varnas, the Jatis were innumerable. In order to maintain social hierarchy, people of various Varnas and Jatis were entitled to perform different occupations and jobs that made them exclusive. In India, untouchability was the by-product of the caste system. It is, therefore, one of the social evils of the caste system. It is a typical Indian phenomenon and is derived from the pure and impure ideology connected with caste. It is against the fundamental principle of humanity. However, it is not just an expression of cultural prejudice but also an unacceptable form of exploitation and injustice that violates the fundamental right of a group of people to live a dignified life and earn their livelihood. The untouchables have always at the bottom of the hierarchy. They were set apart from the rest of the Hindu society and were ever denied normal interaction with their superiors. They were made economically, culturally, socially and politically powerless.

Mahatma Gandhi had taken a lot of efforts to eradicate untouchability and he made it a part of his programme for the attainment of political independence. He was constantly speaking against the practice of untouchability. He struggled hard to abolish casteism and the social stigma of untouchability from the social map of India. Dr. Ambedkar, himself from an untouchable class, also struggled against the practice of untouchability. In a sense, both Gandhi and Ambedkar had made serious efforts to eradicate untouchability. As a social leader, Gandhiji sought to change the hearts of the caste Hindus by moral pressure, whereas Ambedkar continued to work in the field of education and politics in attempting to gain legal rights for the depressed classes. But the ultimate goal of both Gandhiji and Ambedkar was the abolition of untouchability. In this regard Sheshrao Chavan (2001: 28) views: "Gandhiji softened the Hindu heart, Ambedkar awakened self-respect and interest in politics among untouchables, both are considered as the saviours of the untouchables." After Gandhiji's tragic assassination, Ambedkar had taken conscious efforts to form an egalitarian society with equal rights and equal opportunities for the depressed classes. Therefore, in the constitution, Ambedkar had made proper provisions for the social, cultural, economic and political upliftment of the depressed classes or the former untouchables.

Today the Constitution of India provides the blueprint of an egalitarian society. The constitution is not based on the premises of hierarchy, but on the principles of equality. The Indian constitution may be described as secular and multicultural, but it is so in a specific way. The Indian constitution does not reflect only the multicultural reality of India but also protects the rights and interests of the socio-cultural minorities/socio-economically disadvantaged groups. It offers special privileges for the disadvantaged social groups like the untouchables and tribal communities. The Indian constitution promotes genuine pluralism, i.e. the dignified co-existence of all groups recognizing the rights of religious, cultural as well as linguistic minorities. It characterizes conservation and cultivation of such rights as fundamental rights of every citizen of India. Article 29 (1) says that any section of the citizens of India having a distinct language, script or culture of its own shall have the fundamental right to conserve the same. The constitution provides an institutional structure and principles that would allow diverse people to live together as citizens of India. It underlines the ideas of secularism, religious freedom, non-discrimination and equality.

However, the constitution prohibits the practice of untouchability in any form (Article 17) and assures protection to minority cultures by providing them special privileges. In a sense, the constitution promotes and endorses the basic principles of multiculturalism, because India is the world's most complex and comprehensively pluralistic society; it houses a vast variety of castes, tribes, communities, religions, languages, customs and lifestyles. As Harihar Bhattacharyya (2003: 153) says:

> The recent Indian debate on multiculturalism has taken two distinct forms. First, multiculturalism as a state policy has been operative in the growing federalization of its political system, a process that politically accommodates ethnic identities. In this form, multiculturalism is conjoined with federalism. Second, multiculturalism itself, its definition, meaning and implications, has been the subject of discussion among scholars centering around the issues of rights, culture, community and communalism, secularism, religion and so on. Both forms of debate are current today in India.

Therefore, in India, constitutionalism and multiculturalism share a common ideology. Multiculturalism recognizes cultural diversity and appreciates the value of tolerance. It establishes cultural contacts, exchanges cultural ideologies and promotes the value of harmonious coexistence of diverse cultures. As a social ideology, multiculturalism upholds the values of social equality and non-discrimination and welcomes the idea of inclusiveness. It also acknowledges peaceful coexistence of varied cultures with mutual respect and love. Multiculturalism always helps to subvert the dominance of one culture over the others and protects the idea of equality of opportunity and rights of minority/weak cultures. The exponents of multiculturalism admire recognition of identity, may be community, culture, gender or a group, with its distinctiveness. However, the principles of multiculturalism referred to above are not positively reflected in the novel *Untouchable*, because of the rigidity of Indian caste system, which divides people on the basis of colour, occupation, and the wrong notions of purity and pollution. Therefore, from the beginning to the end of the novel, very often, the principles of multiculturalism have been violated.

The caste system in India is probably the main factor, which is responsible for creating the enormous differences between people, and segregates them into different groups or sections like 'Touchables' and 'Untouchables'. Though cultural and ethnic diversity are widely considered as a source of cultural enrichment, they can also generate some crucial social problems. At the societal level, the *touchables* in India form a major community to be a dominant culture, whereas *untouchables*, although their number is very high, are minority cultures. Therefore, throughout the analysis of the novel *Untouchable*, the touchables are considered as the members of a dominant/mainstream culture and the untouchables as the members of subordinate/minority culture. The subordinate status is a basic characteristic of the minority culture. In Untouchable, we see cultural diversity exists without respect and peace. The rift between the dominant and subordinate cultures automatically advances social disharmony in the village of Bulashah. The village represents India's multicultural face but it is infested with tension, injustice, exploitation, deprivation, oppression and disrespect. Mulk Raj Anand sufficiently builds up the atmosphere of inequality and exploitation in his work. The very opening of the novel exposes the sharp demarcations of the multicultural village on the basis of caste, culture, religion, social standing and occupation of the people:

> The outcastes' colony was a group of mud-walled houses that clustered together in two rows, under the shadow both of the town and the cantonment, but outside their boundaries and separate, from them. There lived the scavengers, the leather-workers, the washermen, the barbers, the water carriers, the grass-cutters and other outcastes from Hindu society. A brook ran near the lane, once with crystal-clear water, now soiled by the dirt and filth of the public latrines situated about it, the odour of the hides and skins of dead carcases left to dry on its

> banks, the dung of donkeys, sheep, horses, cows and buffaloes heaped up to be made into fuel cakes, and the biting. Choking, pungent fumes that oozed from its sides. The absence of drainage system had, through the rains of various seasons, made of the quarter a marsh which gave out the most offensive stink. And altogether the ramparts of human and animal refuse that lay on the outskirts of this little colony, and the ugliness, the squalor and the misery which lay within it, made it an 'uncongenial' place to live. (1)

This picture of the outcastes' colony is very naturalistic, but it is also related to the different themes of the novel. The touchables live inside the village and the untouchables outside it in separate quarters. The bisection of the multicultural village based on caste and occupation suggests the approved social disharmony and inequality reinforced by the caste system in India. Indian caste system is hierarchal and it has its roots in the notions of 'purity' and 'impurity' or 'pollution'. These notions of purity and pollution are extremely anti-human and humiliating. The untouchables (dalits) of India are the victims of the Hindu caste system, which is an oppressive social hierarchy, built on the wrong and atrocious principles of purity and pollution, segregation and social exclusion. The dominant culture (politically and socially powerful) has assigned the lowest place in the social ladder to the untouchables to be the slaves and servants of their upper-caste masters. They have to live in segregated dwellings outside the village and are a despised lot. The untouchables' unhygienic situation and filthy life in the village show their miserable condition. The people live in the village, "where there are no drains, no light, no water...where people live among the latrines of the townsmen" (75). They are forced to work in degrading conditions, as they are culturally, socially, economically and politically powerless. Due to their social as well as economic marginalisation, they become the victims of hunger and malnutrition. They always receive base and cruel treatment from the so-called caste Hindus, the members of the dominant culture.

The passage quoted above clearly shows the cultural diversity of the village, but, sadly, it provides no sign of harmonious coexistence, mutual respect and tolerance. On the contrary, it exposes intentional displacement, marginalisation and social exclusion of different weak cultures. Through this passage, Mulk Raj Anand depicts the social reality of the Hindu society in which the groups of untouchables are deprived of their basic human rights and needs. In fact, multiculturalism ensures that all members of the society should live happily with respect, love and harmony. But in this novel, there recurs the vision of social disharmony and disrespect. Therefore, in the opening part of the novel, principles of multiculturalism like social harmony, peaceful co-existence, respect and love towards the other have been violated. As a social doctrine, multiculturalism strengthens democratic principles, which ensure that every citizen has equal rights and the same level of protection and opportunity. But, here we see how untouchables are cunningly and clearly sidetracked by the so-called dominant culture, the so-called controller of social power structures.

Multiculturalism underscores the coexistence of diverse communities and cultures and acknowledges cultural diversity as an inescapable reality in every human society. Cultural diversity includes majority and minority cultures with their distinctiveness and uniqueness. The majority culture is generally placed at an advantageous position as it enjoys power in the public sphere, whereas the minorities, by implication, are usually a deprived lot. The latter have to work harder and their cultures are undervalued. India as a multicultural and multireligious country faces some problems. The dominant culture often exploits and disrespects the subordinate cultures. *Untouchable* exposes the ugly/hideous reality of the Indian caste system and injustice inflicted on the untouchables by the caste Hindus. Throughout their life Bakha and his family work for caste Hindus' hygiene and their purity. But the castes Hindus neither appreciate nor admire their work. On the contrary, they humiliate and disgrace them: "Oh, Bakhya! Oh,

Bakhya! Oh, you scoundrel of a sweeper's son! Come and clean a latrine for me! Someone shouted from without" (7).

What one sees is the dominance of one culture over the others, which leads towards injustice and social unrest. The caste Hindu's foul language indicates his cultural arrogance and supremacy. He seems to treat sweepers as his slaves and orders them to do the menial work. He openly violates the principles of equality and respect and proves to be a 'boss'. His bossy demeanor shows his anti-human approach. Obviously, a dominant culture manages to establish its cultural norms, which are hegemonic, over the others, and tries to impose its cultural domination. The dominant culture oppresses the other weak (minority) cultures and makes them powerless and defenseless. This kind of cultural superiority is evident in the short quoted above. Bakha can sense the unjust superiority of the caste Hindu but has become so passive that is impossible for him to respond.

One of the characteristic features of multiculturalism, as mentioned earlier, is the acknowledgement of the existence of minority cultures. But it also critiques any form of exploitation of the weak culture. But in the novel under discussion, we see how the minority cultures are exploited by the dominant culture. The episode at the public well shows the exploitation of minority cultures in its most hideous form. Pundit Kali Nath, a lecherous and immoral priest, comes to the well. He haughtily looks at the untouchable crowd, but he gets attracted to the beauty of Sohini, Bakha's sister. He is a lecherous fellow and purposefully favors Sohini. He pretends to help her and says: "'Oh, you Lakha's daughter, come here,' 'you have been patient and the reward of patience...is supreme'" (21). Actually he is neither benevolent nor kind-hearted. He only wants to exploit the innocent girl, who is unaware of his lustful intentions. Though she is innocent, she doesn't like the Pundit's favoritism. The other outcastes are suspicious of the Pundit's misbehaviour and false concern for Sohini. But they remain silent, because they are conditioned to believe that they are insignificant and worthless in a caste-ridden Hindu society.

Finally, the lecherous Pundit puts the proposal before Sohini and that is to clean the courtyard of his house:

> Look, why don't you come and clean the courtyard of our house at the temple, called the Brahmin as the girl withdrew. 'Tell your father to send you from to-day.' And he looked long at her, rather embarrassed, his rigid respectability fighting against the waves of amorousness that had begun to flow in his blood. (21-22)

As a member of the minority culture, Sohini remains cold and silent. She doesn't get the evil intentions behind the Pundit's words. Innocently, she puts his proposal before her father and says: "Father, the Pundit of the temple wanted me to clean the family house at the temple" (23). Without any doubt and hesitation her father, Lakha, permits her to go. Perhaps he knows nothing about the Pundit's intention of seducing his daughter. It is said that the caste Hindus strictly follow the notions of purity and impurity. They do not allow the untouchables in the courtyard of their houses, because of the latter's 'low' origins and unclean body. But here we see the irony of the situation. The Pundit himself invites Sohini, the daughter of an untouchable, to his courtyard. He pretends to be a man of compassion or an angel of humanity, but actually he wants to exploit Sohini sexually. Here Mulk Raj Anand exposes the hypocrisy of a caste Hindu who is trying to pollute the 'polluted'. For the sake of his own vulgar physical needs, he exempts for himself the rules of purity and pollution. This kind of duplicity also reveals his mercilessness. Multiculturalism values the dignity and status of the minority cultures, because no culture is wholly worthless; each culture carries some values either social or moral for its members. Though untouchables are labeled as 'polluters' or 'unclean', they have their own moral status and dignity. Therefore, the Pundit's desire to have sexual relation with Sohini is an example of the hypocrisy of the dominant culture that has often exploited and dominated by other minority cultures in the name of purity and pollution. Multiculturalism attempts to empower the weaker sections of society, especially minority cultures. But here instead of empowerment, the dominant culture exploits the minority cultures to intimidate and subdue them. After all, recognizing the dignity and richness of dominant as well as minority cultures depends on the way we look at the world.

When Sohini goes to clean the courtyard of the Pundit's house near the temple, religious activities of singing, offering poojas and aarti are going on there. The caste Hindus are quite busy with their so-called holy and religious performances. Some of them loudly utter words like "Om Shanti Deva" (51) and "Ram Chandar Ki Jai" (52). The devotees create a holy atmosphere of godliness and saintliness. After a while, Bakha comes there to clean the temple premises. The rhythm of the songs attracts him. He instinctively joins his hands and, oblivious of his unworthiness to be there, he begins the "worship of the unknown God" (52). But suddenly a cry disturbs him:

> 'Polluted, polluted, polluted.' A shout rang through the air. He was completely unnerved. His eyes were covered with darkness. He couldn't see anything. His tongue and throat were parched. He wanted to utter a cry, a cry of fear, but his voice failed him. He opened his mouth wide to speak. It was no use. Beads of sweat covered his forehead. He tried to raise himself from the awkward attitude of prostration, but his limbs had no strength left in them. For a second he was as if dead. (52)

Initially, Bakha feels that the religious crowd is against him because of his presence in the temple. So he feels pathetic and becomes subservient. But the situation is quite different. When Sohini begins to clean the courtyard of the Pundit's house, he tries to molest her and makes lustful suggestions. She says, "That man made suggestions to me" (53). In her sense of insecurity, she starts screaming. Pundit Kali Nath, for fear of being found guilty, shouts that Sohini has defiled him. He hides the fact and tries to project his image as a custodian of age-old religious principles. Though other people look at him as a religious man, his misconduct reveals his religious duplicity and pretence. This scene further deepens the irony of the situation. If an untouchable unconsciously touches the caste Hindu, he/she is punished for being a polluter, but if a priest or a pundit touches the untouchable girl for his 'special needs', he is considered neither a defaulter nor a fraud; nor does he feel defilement. This kind of hypocrisy has brought about social unrest in Indian society, because in the hierarchy of Hindu caste system, the caste Hindus are supposed to be at the top and the untouchables are always at the bottom. Due to their cultural dominance, the caste Hindus are not prepared even to listen to Sohini, a victim of the Indian caste system. The Hindu caste system discriminates people and makes them separate on the basis of color, origin, occupation and endogamy. What Anand exposes is the failure of religion in promoting the essential values of multiculturalism.

Multiculturalism further underscores the necessity of providing equal opportunities and rights to all the members of various classes/castes. Opportunities and rights are not to be reserved for a privileged lot who are supposedly 'high-born' and culturally dominant. The rights of the weaker sections should in no way be fewer than those of the members of the major class/caste. Right to education, for example, should be common to all. And the constitution of India ensures this. Education is an instrument of social change at all levels. It sensitizes the human mind and makes man more aware of the meaning of his social existence and identity. In *Untouchable*, we see how minority cultures are deprived of their basic human rights. The basic reason for their deprivation is the lack of opportunity for education, an agent of social change. There are many reasons for Bakha's sufferings and misery. But one of the main reasons for his suffering is the lack of opportunity for education. As an untouchable, Bakha gets no opportunity for education, which he pines for. When Bakha goes to attend his menial work, sometimes he observes the enthusiastic faces of school children, "How beautiful it felt! How nice it must be able to read and write!" (30). Bakha remembers his uncle's story. His uncle wanted to attend school, but his father had denied the opportunity: "...schools were meant for the babus, not for the lowly sweepers" (30). It means untouchables were not allowed to admit their children to schools. The schools were especially established for the upper caste Hindu children.

This is how untouchables were deprived of the opportunities for education. Through the denial of education, the dominant culture in India has established its hegemony over the minds of the untouchables in multiple forms. In fact, education is a basic human right, but millions of untouchables were/are still away from this facility. Though Bakha doesn't get any formal education, he is very curious to learn lessons from a Babu's son. He requests and promises him to pay: "I will pay you an anna per lesson" (32). If Bakha had got the opportunity to study, he would have been a different kind of person, but his caste deprives him of any opportunity for education, a basic human right. Education can bring social change in the lives of the untouchables but the dominant classes do not want such a transformation to take place. The untouchables have been subjected to various social disabilities of extreme forms. They are exploited and are forcibly kept subservient mainly, because they are illiterate. Therefore, Anand seems to imply, it is necessary to provide them education, a dynamic agent of social change and mobility. Bakha represents a minority culture, which remains at the bottom of the caste hierarchy just because it lacks education. On the contrary, the dominant culture enjoys all privileges and opportunities in multicultural societies like India. Bakha's thirst for education is a sign of social change, but Mulk Raj Anand makes him a passive hero, perhaps, because the author wants to suggest that the upper castes maintain their authority by denying education to the less privileged. Education generates power and makes man aware of his rights and identity, may be cultural or individual. In the novel, the members of minority cultures remain in darkness due to the lack of educational opportunities. This keeps them away from their basic rights too. And Anand seems to highlight this lack of opportunity. Because multiculturalism talks of equal rights and opportunities, it has a direct connection with democracy. Both multiculturalism and democracy stand for equality and non-discrimination. They raise questions about accommodating minority cultures, granting them equal status. As Will Kymlicka (1995) says, the accommodation of differences is the essence of true equality. But in India, Hindu caste hierarchy controls the social power structures and unleashes social inequality. As L.S. Ainapur (1992: 160) observes: "The caste system does not embody the Eugenics of modern scientists. It is a social system which embodies the arrogance of selfishness of a perverse section of the Hindus who were superior enough in social status to set in fashion and who had authority to 'force it on their inferiors'." Though the caste system exists almost in all multicultural societies, untouchability in India is related to the notions of purity and pollution. After all, all human beings are more or less aware of their social status. The high caste status is associated with purity and low status with pollution. The untouchables represent in India that section of society which is not only held in the lowest esteem, but which is looked down upon by other castes as 'unclean'. The sweepers are associated with the traditional occupation of cleaning latrines and sweeping public lanes; therefore they are 'unclean'. The involvement of sweepers in such filthy work pushes them to the bottom of the Hindu caste hierarchy, even as their services allow high-status people to maintain their ritual purity. Anand highlights this point in the novel, because they are unclean. The untouchables are not permitted to take water from the public wells:

> The outcastes were not allowed to mount the platform surrounding the well, because if they were never to draw water from it, the Hindus of the three upper castes would consider the water polluted. Nor were they allowed access to the near-by brook as their use of it would contaminate the stream. They had no well of their own because it cost at least a thousand rupees to dig a well in such a hilly town as Bulashah. Perforce they had to collect at the foot of the caste Hindus' well and depend on the bounty of some of their superiors to pour water into their pitchers. (14-15)

Anand here depicts the misery of the untouchable groups in Indian society. Especially, castes Hindus do not allow them to mount the platform of public wells. They have labelled them as 'polluters'. Due to their caste stigma, untouchables are not allowed to enjoy their civil rights. On the contrary, the privileged caste Hindus make their life more dependent on them. Even for water, the basic necessity of human existence, the untouchables have to depend on the mercy of the caste Hindus, the so-called 'clean' people. As stated earlier, multiculturalism promotes the value of social equality and non-discrimination, but here we see restrictions imposed even upon the basic needs. Untouchability is hard to be removed from the minds of the upper class. In this regard P.S. Choondawat (1986: 57) says: "The problem of untouchability, which always remained a part of our society and is deeply rooted in our culture for centuries, will take its own time to die. Today the problem seems to be more of a psychological nature, i.e. people in their day-to-day activities do not manifest directly the behavior which reflects discrimination towards other castes." In fact, multiculturalism respects and celebrates cultural diversity, but the stigma of untouchability makes minority or subordinate cultures more miserable and despondent. Their struggle for water, a basic human need, reveals their social tragedy caused by their 'low' origin. When Sohini goes to fetch water from the public well, she notices the crowd of other outcastes curiously waiting for the arrival of a caste Hindu, who only has the right to draw water. After some time a caste Hindu visitor passes by the well. The miserable outcastes there request him in a chorus:

> Oh, Maharaj! Maharaj! Won't you draw us some water, please? We beg you. We have been a long time, we will be grateful, shouted the chorus of voices as they pressed towards him, some standing up, bending and joining their palms in beggary, others twisting their lips in various attitudes of servile appeal and abject humility, as they remained seated. (18)

The repetition of the word 'Maharaj' shows the rift between the dominant and the subordinate cultures. The touchables' kingly and majestic presence in the society proves their dominance and supremacy, whereas the untouchables' submissiveness clearly suggests their voicelessness and subordination. This kind of class and caste distinction creates communal disharmony and social discontent. The voiceless but needy untouchables have no other option than to request to the caste Hindu who is their present life savior. A thirsty crowd makes a humble and modest request to the caste Hindu but he pays no attention to their request. This is how a rigid caste system creates social inequality in India. Though multiculturalism distinguishes between the majority and minority communities, it argues for the granting of equality to all within the boundaries of both the public and political spheres. Therefore, it is said that equality and non-discrimination are the watchwords of multiculturalism. But here instead of equality and non-discrimination, we see a rift between touchables and untouchables. The dominant culture imposes its cultural hegemony and uniqueness over subordinate cultures and develops prejudices, xenophobia or intolerant sentiments among them. It is believed that living in multicultural societies can be a source of enrichment for everyone, but here minority culture faces problems like social inequality and discrimination. Thus, Anand seems to argue, multicultural society has to recognize cultural diversity mutually, where individuals are neither subjected to the tyrannies of any dominant culture nor the oppression of a dominant group within it. In a decent society there is always a continuous and conscious effort to eliminate humiliation, marginalisation, subordination and to institute rights and dignity in the lives of individuals and groups.

Tolerance, as has already been pointed out, has a prominent place in the discourse on multiculturalism. Traditionally, tolerance has meant acceptance of all forms of cultures, especially the minorities. But in *Untouchable*, tolerance is replaced by intolerance. The pundit's misbehavior with Sohini makes Bakha impatient. But very soon, he becomes a victim of castes Hindus' intolerance and narrow-mindedness. Actually most religions teach tolerance to all people as God's children. But some so-called caste Hindus believe that they are the God's special chosen children. Consequently, religion is misinterpreted by the caste Hindus in different ways. The caste Hindus have no tolerance, they consider a sweeper boy's presence in the temple premises a sin:

> 'Polluted, polluted, polluted!' shouted the Brahmin below. The crowd above him took the cue and shouted after him.... 'Get off the steps, you scavenger! Off with you! You have defiled our whole service you have defiled our temple! Now we will have to pay for the purificatory ceremony. Get down, get away, you dog!' (53)

Bakha comes to know that the caste Hindus are fuming at him because of his unexpected entry into and participation in the religious procession. According to their convention, untouchables are not allowed to participate in the religious rituals like Pooja or Aarti for purity reasons. Anand seems to indicate that all religions are founded on the principles of peace, equality, tolerance, non-discrimination, respect and acceptance of others. The freedom of religion, belief and conscience contributes to the attainment of the goals of social justice and mutual understanding among people. But here religion is used as a weapon of intolerance and narrow-mindedness. The caste Hindus' objection to Bakha's presence in the temple is an example of religious orthodoxy that damages the basic principles of tolerance. It appears that as though Hinduism is monopolized by the caste Hindus, so-called custodians (special children of God), who can restrict untouchables' entry in to the temple and their direct involvement in the religious rituals for purity reasons. No religion has explicitly divided people on the basis of caste, creed, origin or purity and pollution reasons, except Hinduism, as it is controlled by the caste Hindus. It is to look at religion through the lens of purity and impurity. Truly, internal purity is far better than external purity. But the castes Hindus glorify the concept of external purity. The caste Hindus abuse Bakha, as he 'defiles' their holy service. It is ironic that these so-called custodians of religion, rituals and rites are praying to the God who makes no caste-distinctions. Bakha's external impurity is one of the reasons of his humiliation and prohibition of the temple entry. Mahatma Gandhi once said: untouchables are the children of God, but here Bakha is not allowed to enter into the house of God. This is how in India religion discriminates devotees on the basis of their color, caste, origin and social standing. Even today, in some regions, these people are exploited severely in the name of God and religion. This temple scene does not only expose the follies of Indian caste system but also highlights caste Hindus' religious orthodoxy and intolerance. Therefore, to some extent, tolerance, one of the principles of multiculturalism, is violated in the society that the novel depicts.

The concept of multiculturalism centers around the basic assumption that every culture is unique. Yet the assistance of other cultures is necessary for a general understanding of the world. Thus, it is necessary to respect cultural diversity, because each culture carries something valuable for its members. But in the novel the upper castes Hindus are not ready to accommodate and tolerate the minority cultures that are constantly excluded from the mainstream society. Instead of respecting and accommodating minority cultures, they start reacting against their progress and social rise. The dominant culture is intolerant and so worried about the 'uppishness' of the minority cultures:

> 'Don't know what the world is coming to! These swine are getting more and more uppish!' said a little old man. 'One of his brethren who cleans the lavatory of my house, announced the other day that he wanted two rupees a month instead of one rupee, and the food that he gets from us daily.'
>
> 'He walked like a Lat Sahib, like Laften Gornor!' shouted the defiled one. 'Just think, folks, think of the enormity!'
>
> 'Yes, yes, I know,' chimed in a seedy old fellow, 'I don't know what the kalijugs of this age is coming to!'
>
> 'As if he owned the whole street!' exclaimed the touched man. 'The son of a dog!' (39-40)

One by one, the members of the dominant culture express their hostile attitude towards the untouchables' social 'uppishness' and their enterprise of having social change in terms of economic, social and cultural equality. Through their remarks, the members of the dominant culture are making attempts to reassert their hegemony and power which they have maintained for centuries. They feel restless and are surprised by the untouchables' boldness, their behavior, style and courage to demand more money. In a sense, the mainstream class is not ready to admit and acknowledge the social change being advanced by the minority cultures. For centuries, the upper castes have been exploiting the minorities for their own sake, in the name of purity and impurity. But now the *kalijugs*, as Mulk Raj Anand feels, may bring social change. But the sign of social change might be disturbing to the so-called upper caste Hindus who are worried about the untouchables' awareness of their cultural identity and their social upliftment: "They are getting more and more uppish" (65). Consequently, intolerance of the dominant culture brings social inequality and it leads to social conflict and friction.

Untouchability is one of the root causes of the outcastes' social marginalisation. The term 'untouchability' carries with it connotations of degradation, humiliation and inhuman oppression in Indian society. In *Untouchable*, Mulk Raj Anand pictures the plight of the untouchables. Anand's Bakha is universal in that he represents the millions of untouchables and their predicament. The novel depicts the glaring evil of untouchability, the root cause of social marginalisation in Indian society. The stigma of untouchability makes Bakha too pathetic and weak. He is easily insulted and marginalized by the upper caste Hindus like the shopkeeper, confectioner, Lalaji and others. When Bakha passes through the street, he comes across a betel-leaf shop where he sees "a number of packets of Red-Lamp" (33). He wishes to have a cigarette packet:

> He haulted suddenly, and facing the shopkeeper with great humility, joined his hands and begged to know where he could put a coin to pay for a packet of 'Red-Lamp.' The shopkeeper pointed to a spot on the board near him. Bakha put his anna there. The betel-leaf-seller dashed some water over it from the jug with which he

> sprinkled the betel leaves now and again. Having thus purified it he picked up the nickel piece and threw it into the counter. Then he flung a packet of 'Red-Lamp' cigarettes at Bakha, as a butcher might throw a bone to an insistent dog sniffing round the corner of his shop. (33-34)

The above extract exposes the prevailing untouchability as a severe problem that marginalizes a helpless young man like Bakha. The shopkeeper's act of purifying a 'polluted coin' speaks a lot about the severity of untouchability. Untouchability emerges out of the caste system. It was practiced, and is being practiced even now in most of the villages in India. The castes Hindus sensitively attribute untouchability to pollution, which is the result of the occupational patterns of the untouchables who are involved in filthy and unclean work. Therefore, after purifying the coin, the shopkeeper picks it up and then flings a packet of cigarette at Bakha, like a butcher throws a bone to an insistent dog. The shopkeeper insults Bakha only, because of the latter's 'low' origin and because he bears the stigma of untouchability. This kind of social marginalisation is quite unbearable. He treats Bakha neither as a customer nor as a client but as an untouchable, a socially marginal polluter. The insulting of Bakha is a result of 'pollution', a derogatory word that is permanently attached to untouchability.

A series of degrading and disgraceful events chase Bakha throughout the day. When Bakha crosses the street, he comes across a sweet mart. His mouth begins to water for the sweets covered with silver paper on a tray. He thought: "'Eight annas in my pocket', 'dare I buy some sweets'?" (36). Without his father's fright, he decides to taste the sweets. He goes near the sweet mart and asks the confectioner for some jalebi. The confectioner is more caste prejudiced and intolerant than the shopkeeper. He directs his assistant to splash some water on the coin being placed by Bakha. After the coin purification ceremony, he throws a packet of jalebi at Bakha, who catches it "like a cricket ball" (37). In a mixed mood of happiness and insult, Bakha unfolds the paper in which the jalebi is wrapped.

He tastes the sweets and walks through the street by looking at the signboards. Bakha, in that joyful experience of tasting jalebi, unconsciously touches a caste Hindu Lalaji, who slaps and humiliates him:

> 'Keep to the side of the road, you, low-caste vermin!' he suddenly heard someone shouting at him. 'Why don't you call, you swine, and announce your approach! Do you know you have touched me and defiled me, you cockeyed son of a low-legged scorpion! Now I will have to go and take bath to purify myself. And it was a new dhoti and shirt I put on this morning!' (38)

Bakha is mortified and the wrath of the caste Hindu, who expects the usual warning call of Bakha's approach, almost benumbs him. Lallaji abuses and slaps Bakha for touching him. Bakha stands amazed and embarrassed, unable to utter a single word. Instinctively, he joins his hands and tries to apologize. But Lallaji is not appeased. He says: "Dirty dog! Son of a bitch!" (38). Lallaji deliberately addresses Bakha as a 'swine', 'cockeyed son', and Bakhya, instead of Bakha, as he knows his social status. His address is deliberately contrived to crush the untouchables under the weight of subjugation and psychological oppression. Though he humiliates Bakha, still Bakha stands with his hands joined. This indicates his meekness and timidity due to his low caste origin. Furthermore, Lallaji inhumanly beats him and calls him a "careless, irresponsible swine!" (40). However, the crowd simply gets delighted and does not even think of rescuing him from that helpless situation. The inhumanity of the crowd is obvious evidence to the hostile society around the sweeper boy, who continuously struggles against his social marginalisation. Luckily, a tonga-wallah, a member of the same class, comes there to rescue Bakha and sees his pitiable condition: "Bakha's turban fell off and the Jalebi in the paper bag in his hand were scattered in the dust" (41). This tragic scene indicates how caste Hindus dictate terms to and dominate the members of minority cultures, who are mute sufferers due to their social marginalisation, in the name of caste and religion. It is a social irony that the so-called 'patriots' (caste Hindus) of India show lip sympathy towards the untouchables while secretly discriminate people on the basis of caste and occupations. Sometimes touchables demand political rights, but the so-called caste Hindus are not ready to give social rights and equal status to the untouchables. Therefore, social equality and fraternity remain a mirage in Indian society.

Throughout the day Bakha tolerates many offenses. When he goes to play hockey with his friends, belonging to different strata of society, he is insulted by a lady for the offence of touching her son. Actually Ram Charan, another friend of Bakha, injures her son. Bakha notices the seriousness of the boy's wound. Immediately, he picks up the boy and goes to his house. Without any confirmation, the lady scolds Bakha: "You eater of your masters, you dirty sweeper! What have you done to my son?" (106). Bakha is confused and bewildered due to this sudden verbal attack. He tries to open his mouth to explain things, but the lady goes on humiliating him: "'You have defiled my house', 'Get away, get away'" (106). Bakha fails to convince her. He feels dejected and blames his fate as a marginal untouchable. As J. Bheemaiah (2005: 19) views: "Bakha carries the yoke of insult meted out to him by the caste Hindus. His heart is injured by the derogatory expression of an upper caste woman who abuses him for rescuing her wounded child. The rescuing operation is also 'a sin by touch' in this caste-prejudiced society. There are many incidents which constitute Bakha's humiliation." It is seen that throughout the novel, the protagonist Bakha suffers a lot due to the stigma of caste, a major reason for his social marginalisation and humiliation.

Bakha is not the only victim of caste-prejudice and hatred in Hindu society. His father, Lakha, has also been a victim. Comparatively, Lakha's public disgrace and degradation are more shocking than that of his son. For instance, he narrates a heart-rending story of his degradation, when he goes to the doctor with his son (Bakha). Once his son was seriously ill, so he went to the doctor. But nobody was there to attend to the child. He was standing there expectantly for an hour. Finally he lifted the curtain of the door and straightway went in and caught the doctor's feet: "Still there is a little breath left in my child's body, Hakim ji, I shall be your slave all my life" (72). He was shivering due to his tension about his son's life. Suddenly he heard a roaring sound:

> 'Bhangi! (Sweeper) Bhangi!' There was an uproar in the medicine house. People began to disperse hither and thither as the Hakim's feet had become defiled. He was red and pale in turn, and shouted at the highest pitch of his voice: 'Chandal! (Low-caste) by whose orders have you come here? And then you join hands and hold my feet and say you will become my slave forever. You have polluted hundreds of rupees worth of medicine. Will you pay for it'? (73)

The above extract displays touchables' caste phobia. The touchable crowd suddenly roars only because of Lakha'a entry into the dispensary. It's a human tragedy that people think more about the caste and less about human life. Actually Lakha's son is struggling for his life, but the so-called '(im) pure' people are worried about the defilement of the Hakim's feet. It is sheer nonsense to look at the people through the dusted lenses of purity and impurity. His professional ethics should force the Hakim to treat the boy immediately. But he only terrorizes Lakha who has defiled his feet. The Hakim is more anxious about the polluted medicine and less serious about the boy. This shows how caste hatred in India is deep-rooted among the caste Hindus. The Hakim's caste phobia signals the loss of humanism, equality, brotherhood and social justice. It is said that Hakims are saviors of human life, but this caste-conscious fellow gives more importance to the notions of purity, impurity, defilement and pollution. Mulk Raj Anand notices how caste determines and decides the place of man in Indian society. It is a major hurdle in cultivating the idea of harmonious coexistence of the people with their differences. In a sense, the untouchables have been economically and socially deprived, forced to live on the fringes of society, and excluded from basic advantages such as education and health services. Therefore, equality does not mean treating every one the same.

But it means providing the right service to all people regardless of their caste, religion and social standing.

Multiculturalism ensures that all the members of a society, regardless of their caste and religion, have equal opportunity to reach their full potential with dignity and respect. But so far as Bakha and his father are concerned, the dominant culture disrespects and marginalizes them, because of their degrading and filthy occupation and stigma of untouchability. Due to caste Hindus' prejudice against the untouchables, Bakha and his father cannot enjoy their social freedom. Multiculturalism strengthens democracy and it guarantees equal rights and the same level of protection and opportunity to everyone. In Bakha's case, nobody supports and treats him as an equal member of the society. Especially the shopkeeper, confectioner and Lallaji treat him like a stray dog. They are not ready to acknowledge Bakha's freedom, right to smoke a cigarette and buy/enjoy sweets in the street. Bakha's father also suffers due to his low origin. It obviously shows how the dominant culture is a major hurdle in the way of untouchables' lives. They need constant struggle against their social marginalisation, inequality, disrespect and so on. Untouchables are the most marginalized, degraded, downtrodden, exploited and the least benefited in Indian society. They are socially, culturally, economically and politically subjugated and marginalized only because of their caste.

Economic marginalisation, social exclusion, deprivation and isolation with reference to some classes are some of the disturbing features of Indian society, particularly that of Hindu society. In fact, all these features are interlinked. Economic marginalisation involves the process through which individuals or groups are wholly excluded from the economic opportunities, which help them to minimize the level of their poverty. In India, untouchables are diplomatically excluded from economic facilities and opportunities. Obviously, their economic marginalisation generates adverse consequences in terms of human rights, deprivation, poverty and isolation. Therefore, the roots of their poverty lie in their economic marginalisation and social exclusion. Poverty is one of the reasons of Bakha's desolation and misery. It is said that poverty knows no status and dignity. It always resides in the untouchables' 'roofless' houses.

Bakha's next unpleasant experience also suggests the depth of his poverty. When he goes from house to house to collect bread, he gets no response from anyone. Standing at their doorsteps, he shouts: "Bread for the sweeper, mother; bread for the sweeper" (59). But nobody pays attention. He feels tired and sits down on the wooden platform of a house in a lane. After sometime, a sadhu comes there shaking the bangles on his arms and cries: "Bham, bham, bhole Nath" (62). The sadhu's peculiar chant attracts two women who start rushing to the terraces of their housetops. Both are quite eager to meet the sadhu and feed him. "I am bringing the food sadhuji" (62), one of them says. When she comes with the food, she sees the sweeper's body knotted up on the wooden platform outside her house. In her fury, she shouts at Bakha: "You have defiled my house" (63). Her caste hatred is at its peak and it disheartens Bakha. Immediately she goes upstairs and throws some bread: "Vay Bakhya, take this. Here's your bread coming down" (65). Her act of throwing bread from upstairs shows her inhumanity and heartlessness. She treats the sadhu with piety and Bakha with inhumanity and degradation. Bakha, like a beggar, picks up the bread and wraps it in a duster with the other bread he has received. This one more fresh insult makes him more furious. As we know beggars have neither choice nor sense of dignity, therefore, they have to cope with the situation, which always brings them disgrace and humiliation. As Binod Mishra (2005: 2-3) says: "Anand's characters are born and bred in poverty. They are born to earn their own bred but the age-old tradition of keeping them under the yoke of dejection and debauchery born of exploitation deprive them of their dignity of labour...their exploitation by their masters is undoubtedly man's crime against man."

Here we notice how the Sadhu and Bakha have received different forms of treatment from the same woman. The sadhu's soft call pleases her, whereas Bakha's presence on the wooden platform, according to her casteist belief, spoils the purity of her house. The woman badly humiliates Bakha, as she knows he is a sweeper and an outcaste. But she welcomes the sadhu, a model of purity for her, and treats him in a proper way. In a sense, she has regards for a lazy, deceptive sadhu and hates the toiling Bakha. In this context, Premila Paul (1983: 15) remarks: "The Hindu housewives favour the lazy sadhus with hot vegetable curry and rice whereas they fling thin, stale slices of bread to the laboring class." This kind of variation in treatment indicates her mental poverty to exclude the outcaste who is made for beggary and favours the sadhu, the member of a fake culture. Though the untouchables do menial work, their struggle for food never ends, because of their economic marginalisation. As J. Bheemaiah (2005: 58) says: "The improvement in the economic conditions of the untouchables is a pre-requisite for their emancipation from traditional bondage. Depressed economic conditions lead to illiteracy, social immobility, and loss of personal freedom which eventually affect the development of human personality." Multiculturalism promotes inclusiveness and denounces social exclusion and economic marginalisation. It is the responsibility of all Indians to support all groups and cultures and guarantee them equal treatment and economic opportunity. This inclusive approach will definitely help one to contribute to the social and economic life of India. It also makes possible to free oneself from any kind of discrimination based on race, culture, religion, gender or place of birth. Thus, the multicultural policy of inclusiveness provides a framework for maximizing the social, cultural and economic benefits that cultural diversity brings to all Indians. However, as of now, what one witnesses is the untouchables' economic marginalisation, one of the root causes of their misery and sufferings.

Bakha returns home with a heavy heart, with regret and a sense of humiliation. In his disgusted mood, he finds excuses for not bringing home sufficient food: "I don't know the people in the town very well, and I didn't call at all the houses for food" (68). This remark upsets his father. Lakha, an old-time untouchable, knows all kinds of mortification and degradation. So he tries to support his son mentally and makes him aware of the social evils being imposed on them by the caste Hindus. As he says: "You should try and get to know them. You have got to work for them all your life, my son, after I die" (68). Lakha's every word reflects the subordinate status of minorities and their helplessness and defenselessness in Indian society. They are only made for 'others' (caste Hindus). For centuries, the minorities have mortgaged their lives for the service of others. Therefore, Lakha, the old-time untouchable tries to convince his son of the social fact of their subordinate status in society due to caste. But Bakha, a boy of self-respect and identity, is quite restless about his subordinate status in society on the basis of his caste. He is terrified by the horrible prospect of all the future days of service with insult and subordinate status in society. A sensitive Bakha feels suffocated and writhes in the feelings of degradation and subordination. His suppressed feelings come out like this:

> They insulted me this morning; they abused me because as I was walking along a man happened to touch me. He gave me a blow.... 'But, father, what is the use?' Bakha shouted. They would ill-treat us even if we shouted. They think we are mere dirt because we clean their dirt. That pundit in the temple tried to molest Sohini and then came shouting: 'Polluted, polluted.' The woman of the house in the silversmith's gulley threw the bread at me from the fourth story. I won't go down to the town again. I have done with this job. (70)

Bakha takes stock of all the humiliation that he has received throughout the day. He furiously attacks the caste Hindus' dehumanizing tendencies to sidetrack the minorities and make their own centrality sounder, as they can easily control the power structures of society. The caste is one of the reasons for Bakha's subordinate status in society. And according to the social hierarchy, his social standing causes him mental agony and physical sufferings. He is abused and beaten in the street by the caste Hindus, as they are well aware of his insignificance and caste-associated subordinate status in society. Bakha says to his father how their menial work brings disgrace and makes them subordinates in society. In his desperate mood, he refers to the pundit's meanness and nastiness. He angrily says that nobody objects to the pundit's amorous behavior with Sohini because 'they' know she belongs to the lower strata of society. These episodes upset him. Actually the woman's act of throwing bread at Bakha shows her heartlessness, egotism and inhumanity. But nobody speaks about her lack of concern for him. The caste Hindus take pride in claiming their high and superior status and, therefore, they do not oppose the social evil of caste system. As a result of their pride and arrogance, now a days, the minorities have started making special demand for equal social status and respect regardless of their caste, culture or occupation. Multiculturalism assumes that a multicultural society is composed not only of individuals but also of groups of dominant and minority cultures. But all cultures, including the dominant and minority, have to respect each other. Bakha's father openly admits the master-slave relations between the dominant and minority cultures. Though he knows untouchables are the victims of caste system, he mutely accepts it as a social fact. Perhaps he knows the futility of challenging the dominant culture. Therefore, he appeals to his son, let 'them' be respected because 'they' are our masters. Finally, Lakha succeeds in convincing his son and makes him leave the idea of challenging the dominant culture. For Mulk Raj Anand, literature should be an interpretation of the truth of people's lives. Therefore, he extinguishes Bakha's idea of revolt against the dominant culture and shows the rift between the dominant culture and minority cultures as a social truth in the caste Hindu Indian society. And the dominance of one culture over other will be a constant practice in India. Though multiculturalism respects cultural diversity, it also shows that mere presence of many, plural cultures and communities are not enough. Within a democracy differences must not be a source of discrimination. It must be acknowledged and accommodated within a democratic polity. But in the novel, the dominant culture is more rigid and stiff, whereas minority cultures are quite flexible and are ready to respect and accommodate the dominant culture. This kind of one-sided respect will not be helpful in cultivating the ideal of an egalitarian society.

It is said that our universal identity as human beings is our primary identity and is more fundamental than any other identity. Though identity is of different kinds, everyone should be recognized for his or her unique identity may be as individual, caste, cultural, ethnic, religious, or national. Here, we are more concerned with Bakha's caste identity and less with his individual identity, because recognition of caste/community identity is one of the major issues on the agenda of multiculturalism. Multiculturalism values both caste and community identity and acknowledges the importance of the 'distinctiveness' of those castes and communities. Bakha, a young sweeper protagonist of eighteen suffers a lot due to the stigma of untouchability. Though Bakha is a sweeper, he has some rare human virtues like sincerity, loyalty and efficiency. As E.M. Forster points out in the novel's preface: "Bakha is a real individual, lovable, thwarted, sometimes grand, sometimes weak, and thoroughly Indian." He is very much conscious of his caste identity and low social standing. His survival does not rely so much on his inner strength as an individual; rather, it is dependent on the action of the others that surround him, especially the members of the dominant culture. Bakha represents the whole minority culture, which is a victim of continuous exclusion from the mainstream of Indian society. The castes Hindus exploit untouchables in different ways. They fail to recognize them as equals in human society. In this regard, V. Thanuavalingam (2001: 45) says: "In *Untouchable* the conflict is presented in the opening page itself, viz., Bakha craves the life style of the Tommies who treat him 'as a human being', and he longs for social recognition from others." When Bakha does the menial work of cleaning latrines in the barracks of a British regiment, he is caught by the glamour of the "white man's life" (2). Bakha's love for modernity is his attempt to protect himself against the evil of caste system. He wants to wear the sahib's clothes and speak his language. He starts dreaming to be a sahib, a superior man. He tries to imitate them in everything. He attempts to adopt the fashion of the Tommies and desires to live like them. His desire of becoming a sahib gives him a little mental relief. He appreciates British Tommies' non-discriminatory egalitarian approach of giving equal treatment to all human beings. He dreams of being a different kind of man and says: "'I will look like a sahib', and 'I shall walk like them'" (3). He values white men's humanism and tries to imitate their way of life. This kind of revolutionary change he wants to undergo, because of caste Hindus' discriminatory attitude towards the untouchables. In this regard, P.K. Rajan (1986: 15) says: "Bakha, as an untouchable, seeks his freedom in a feudal society with its unquestionable faith in the infallibility of caste discrimination, with its hypocrisy, cruelty, deceit and inhumanity."

Both Bakha and Sohini are victims of different social evils that prevail in India. Though Bakha is deserted and insulted by the caste Hindus, he wants to teach the Pundit, his sister's seducer a lesson. When Sohini narrates a brief story of Pundit's tomfoolery, Bakha rushes to the middle of the courtyard and drags his sister behind him. He searches the figure of the Pundit in the crowd. His eyes look wild and red. He repeatedly asks Sohini: "Tell me, tell me, that he didn't do anything to you!" (54). But Sohini weeps and says: "...he came and held me by my breast" (54). This revelation makes Bakha more furious. As P.K. Rajan (1992: 106) observes: "Anand's protagonist fights against a hostile environment to discover a world of new freedom. The novel presents to us the drama of the gradual emergence of an aggressive mind, lit with a new knowledge, from an original psychic state of ignorance. Aggression, in this case, results from external social conditions." In his fury, Bakha abuses the Pundit: "The son of a Pig" (55). Again he rushes to the courtyard for locating the Pundit, but Sohini controls him: "No, no. Come back. Let's go away" (55). His rebellious spirit gets extinguished immediately due to his caste consciousness and social marginalisation. Sohini knows Bakha's attempt to teach a lesson to the Pundit will be futile. She knows quite well that downtrodden cultures can be easily victimized under the notions of purity and pollution. Therefore, she compels Bakha to get rid of the idea of revenge. A sense of social insecurity and injustice disturbs both of them. Bakha gets disturbed because of the unbridled power of the dominant culture that moulds, directs and controls the lives of minority or subordinate cultures. Inwardly, he thinks about his passive existence in a society where the wall between the dominant and minority cultures is too thick. He pities his own insignificant and trivial existence in his society. His helpless existence is depicted thus:

> A superb specimen of humanity he seemed whenever he made the high resolve to say something, to go and do something, his fine form rising like a tiger at bay. And yet there was a futility written on his face. He could not overstep the barriers, which the conventions of his superiors had built up to protect their weakness against him. He could not invade the magic circle, which protects a priest from attack by anybody, especially by a low-caste man. So in the highest moment of his strength, the slave in him asserted itself, and he lapsed back, wild with torture, biting his lips, ruminating his grievances. (56)

In *Untouchable*, Mulk Raj Anand exposes certain facts concerning Indian society where there is a constant clash and disagreement between the dominant and the subordinate or minority cultures. Bakha, a boy of self-respect and identity, wishes to challenge the traditional dominant culture that makes him socially and culturally frail and weak. He silently cries: "Why didn't I go and kill that hypocrite" (56). But he remains inactive, because he is culturally conditioned to accept his marginalized status in society, where dominant culture easily sidelines him in the name of either religion or caste. The injustice meted out to him causes his blood boil and this causes unrest in him, but the age-old ingrained caste stigma makes him 'impotent'. He knows the futility of his life because of his low caste origin. In a sense, he is the member of a 'broken' culture that doesn't dare to overstep the barriers of caste and culture made by his 'superiors', the so-called members of the dominant culture. As Ambuj Sharma (2004: 74) says: "Bakha was surprised to notice a lot of differences between the approach of Hindus and non-Hindus, Muslims, Christians, towards the low castes. Bakha's heart was filled with disgust and hatred for the high caste Hindus for exploiting and torturing all the untouchables."

It is a social tragedy that the dominant culture shields these barriers for the sake of hiding their weaknesses. Practically it is very difficult, even in post-modern India, to invade the vicious circle of the dominant culture as drawn for itself. It humiliates and disgraces the lives of low-caste people, members of minority cultures. Indian elites (upper caste Hindus) have built a national culture that is based on the invisibility and marginalisation of minority groups. Consequently, the minorities have been both devalued as well as marginalized. Their world-views are sidelined and downgraded by the so-called dominant culture. Therefore, due to the governance of the dominant culture, Bakha remains weak and tolerates the strokes of humiliation, injustice and inequality without any grievances. Actually multiculturalism reduces the barriers such as discrimination and exclusiveness. But here we see how the dominant culture strengthens the walls between castes and communities and violates the principles of multiculturalism such as equality and justice.

Mulk Raj Anand exposes the grim realities of the social life in India. He pictures the evil of caste system and creates awareness in his readers about the dehumanizing social evils. In this regard, C.J. George (2000: 19) says: "To Mulk Raj Anand, casteism is an age-old lie made by the powerful and wicked in society to uphold discrimination. His prime concern as a social critic is to remove caste system as it damages social cohesion by giving certain sections of society an unfair advantage over others permanently." This obviously means that prevailing casteism in India damages the lives of millions of untouchables who are ignorant about their own identities. After a street drama of humiliation, Bakha inwardly thinks about his misery. He blames the caste-ridden society of India where untouchables are inhumanly oppressed and compressed in the name of purity and pollution. Bakha tolerates the shocks of humiliation and dishonor. His social position as an untouchable illuminates the inner walls of his mind. He realizes that though he possesses good qualities like any human being-head and heart, flesh and blood, still in the eyes of the world, he is an untouchable. Therefore, consciously he shouts aloud the warning shouts to announce his approach: "Posh, posh, sweeper coming" (42). In this regard, K.N. Sinha (1989: 23) observes: "It is not the consciousness of men that determines their existence, but, on the contrary, it is their social existence that determines their consciousness." Bakha comes to know that how the hypocrite caste Hindus twist, torture and silence him. He recognizes the wickedness and inequality of the society in which he is placed. To Bakha, every moment now seems to be an endless age of misery and suffering. Hence, in one of private moments of anguish, he inwardly raises the question of his caste identity:

> The cruel crowd! All of them abused, abused, abused. Why are we always abused? The sentry inspector and the Sahib that day abused my father. They always abuse us. Because we are sweepers. Because we touch dung. They hate dung. I hate it too. That's why I came here. I was tired of working on the latrines every day. That's why they don't touch us, the high-castes...for them I am a sweeper, sweeper-untouchable! Untouchable! Untouchable! That's the world! Untouchable! I am an Untouchable! (43)

In Bakha's heart there is now a burning rage. Neither the crowd nor a passer by consoles him. So he becomes impatient and blames his low caste origin in Indian society. Actually the untouchables' menial work needs to be appreciated socially. From dawn to dusk, the sweepers work without any complaint. But nobody considers and appreciates their destitution and hardship. In this regard, Amitabh Roy (2005: 103) rightly says: "It is an irony of civilization that people who work hardest to produce riches suffer the most and fare the worst. They are looked down upon and treated shabbily by the powerful." Instead of appreciation, the dominant culture humiliates and disgraces them as 'unclean'. Therefore, Bakha, in his frenzy, directs his questions to the caste-prejudiced members of the dominant culture who brutally treat him in the street and marginalize him as an outcaste. His pointed question: "Why are we always abused?" indicates his righteous anger against the hypocrite caste Hindus who promote casteism. For the sake of their self-interest, they categorize people in the name of caste, purity, religion and occupation. Bakha tries to find out the reasons of all the events, which take place in the course of that day. He repeats the word 'untouchable' several times and mentally translates the word 'sweeper' as 'untouchable'. Finally he realizes how caste is one of the root causes of his misery. But he has no other option than to accept the unfairness and injustice inflicted on him by the caste Hindus. It is quite ironical that the caste Hindus glorify Hinduism as a religion of humanity. But at the practical level, the so-called custodians of Hinduism violate the principle of humanity and treat the untouchables like animals. As it is often said, Hinduism is indirectly responsible for the brutal segregation of Indian society. In this connection C.J. George (2000: 40) says: "Casteism is a social practice and no Hindu religious leader of any merit and significance would admit it as part of his religion. Giving a place to casteism in Hindu religion is done by certain wolves in sheep's skin for certain privileges and advantages. "It means casteism in India is a chronic social disease that segregates Indian society. As a principle, multiculturalism recognizes that all human beings are born free and are equal in dignity and rights, and have the capacity to contribute constructively to the development of their societies. Instead of respecting Bakha as an individual, he is left to suffer and depression. Actually his honesty and sincerity of work contribute a lot to human society, but his caste stigma demoralizes and disheartens him.

Bakha suffers too much in one day's time. He cries in exasperation: "Unlucky, unlucky day! What have I done to deserve all this?" (110). He repeats the word 'unlucky' as he blames his misfortune. Patiently he can sum up the causes of the entire day's sufferings and anguish. Still he controls the burning flames of anger and remains passive. However, he is conscious of the emptiness within him. Luckily Colonel

Hutchinson comes there and puts his hand round his shoulders and says: "Tum udas (You are sad)" (113). Bakha is surprised to hear the broken Hindustani of an Englishman. He salutes the sahib who asks him: "What has happened? Are you ill?" (114). This is the first moment in Bakha's life when he is sympathetically addressed by a 'superior'. He feels confused and embarrassed by the flood of kindness and compassion. Hutchinson tells him about Christianity, a more accommodative religion than other religions. However, the gracious treatment from the sahib, who wants to convert him, confuses Bakha. Innocently he asks the sahib: "Who is Yessuh Messih, Sahib?" (116). The sahib replies to him that he is the God of 'all'. This reply has its influence on Bakha as he learns that Christianity is more humanitarian than the caste blind Hinduism. Out of curiosity, Bakha goes on asking different questions related to the existence of God and its relation with human society. The Colonel tries to satisfy Bakha by making ideas simpler as he wants to convert Bakha to Christianity. Of course, conversion to Christianity may be liberation from the casteist Hindu society. The Colonel almost compels Bakha to embrace Christianity. He tells Bakha about the sacrifice by Jesus for human liberation. As he says: "He sacrificed himself for us, for the rich and the poor, for the Brahmin and the Bhangi" (120). In comparison with other religions, Christianity respects the idea of a casteless society and promotes the value of equality and brotherhood. But Bakha does not wish to be converted. Mulk Raj Anand compares two religions—Hinduism and Christainity and indicates that no religion will liberate the minority cultures that are in all sense crushed under the heavy weight of dominant culture's mean acts like discrimination, deprivation, oppression, suppression and humiliation.

At the end of the day, Bakha learns that Mahatma Gandhi is going to deliver a speech at Golbagh. He goes to Golbagh, as "The word 'Mahatma' was like a magical magnet to him" (126). He dissolves in the crowd without even remembering the fact of his being an untouchable. Actually he touches a few, but nobody notices, as they are all in a hurry to listen to

Mahatma Gandhi's words. India's multicultural face is revealed in these lines:

> Men, women and children of all the different races, colours, castes and creeds, were running towards the oval. There were Hindu lallas from the piece-goods market of Bulashah, smartly dressed in silks; there were Kashmiri Muhammadans from the local carpet factories, immaculately clad in white cotton; there were the rough Sikh rustics from the near-by villages swathed in handspun cloth, staves in their hands and loads of shopping on their backs; there were fierce-looking red cheeked Pathans shirted in red stuff, followers of Abdul Gaffar Khan, the frontier revolutionary; there were black-faced Indian Christian girls from the Salvation Army colony, in short coloured skirts, blouses and aprons; there were people from the outcastes' colony, whom Bakha recognized in the distance, but whom he was too rushed to greet; there was here and there a stray European—there was everybody going to meet the Mahatma, to pay homage to Mohandas Karam Chand Gandhi. (126-27)

Perhaps, this is the only scene in the novel that perfectly shows the multicultural face of India. The people from various cultures and religions assemble there to listen to Mahatma Gandhi's spiritual message for the 'masses'. As the scene suggests Mahatma Gandhi is only a single thread that can bind all cultures and religions together. He is a messenger of fraternity, non-violence, social equality, peace and justice. Mulk Raj Anand, therefore, glorifies the image of Gandhi, as he knows that Gandhian philosophy is perhaps only a source of comfort to the untouchable classes, which have been constantly suffering from the social evils like untouchability, discrimination, deprivation, social marginalisation and injustice. In that sense, Mahatma Gandhi is a genuine proponent of multiculturalism, who has struggled to form a harmonious society with peace and love. Therefore, for the untouchables, Mahatma Gandhi is like a 'God' toiling to eradicate untouchability from the essentially multicultural map of India. Hence, the assembled multicultural crowd indicates Mahatma Gandhi's popularity as a social leader who struggles for the equality of the masses and the establishment of the basic principles of multiculturalism. However, in the huge crowd, Bakha, one of the listeners, thinks: "It is good that I came!" (132). He asks himself: "Is he really going to talk about the outcastes, about us, about Chota, Ram Charan, my father and me?" (132). Of course, Bakha is quite eager to listen to Mahatma Gandhi, a supporter of minority cultures, especially untouchables. Mahatma Gandhi begins his speech with: "I regard untouchability as the greatest blot on Hinduism" (137). Mahatma goes on talking about the deprivation and sufferings of the untouchables. The following emotional declaration moves Bakha:

> If I have to be born, I should wish to be born as an untouchable, so that I may share their sorrows, sufferings and the affronts leveled at them, in order that I may endeavor to free myself and them from their miserable condition. (138)

Mahatma Gandhi's speech appeals to Bakha, as he is also one of the suffering untouchables. Bakha begins to adore Mahatma Gandhi in his heart. He attentively listens to each word of Gandhi, but sometime feels unconvinced about Gandhi's statement, "that the Hindus are not sinful by nature, they are sunk in ignorance" (139). This statement confuses Bakha, as he firmly believes that the caste Hindus are the real social culprits who divide people in the name of caste, religion and occupations. However, Bakha is overwhelmed by Mahatma's emotional appeal to the caste Hindus: "All public wells, temples, roads, schools, sanatoriums, must be declared open to the untouchables" (139). Continuing his speech, Gandhi says that the untouchables must purify their own lives first, and must cultivate the habits of cleanliness. At this point Bakha feels that the Mahatma is not fair as he directly blames the untouchables' impurity. Throughout his speech, Mahatma tries to convince the audience that untouchables should be set free from the stigma of untouchability, a social evil. As he says, social change depends on the mentality of the so-called 'elites' who categorize people and exploit them for their own sake. For Gandhi, untouchables are a part and parcel of the Hindu society, and Hindus are solely responsible for the social marginalisation of the untouchables. It is their moral responsibility to rehabilitate them in society. Each word of the concluding part of the Mahatma's speech seems to convey Bakha's own feelings of horror and indignation at the ill treatment of the untouchables by the caste Hindus. Till the end of the speech, many times Bakha gets confused as he expects a practical solution for his problems. After Gandhi's speech, the crowd disperses on a note of happiness and gladness. On his way back, Bakha hears a dissident voice: "'Gandhi is a humbug', 'He is a fool. He is a hypocrite'" (141). Perhaps, the commentator doesn't like Mahatma's less practical and more philosophical views. After a while, a young poet, Iqbal Nath comes there and attracts the people by exposing the social facts:

> Well, we must destroy caste; we must destroy the inequalities of birth and unalterable vocations. We must recognize an equality of rights, privileges and opportunities for everyone. The Mahatma didn't say so, but the legal and sociological basis of caste having been broken down by the British-Indian penal code, which recognizes the rights of every man before a court, caste is now mainly governed by profession. When the sweepers change their profession, they will no longer remain untouchables. And they can do that soon, for the first thing we will do when we accept the machine, will be to introduce the machine which clears dung without anyone having to handle it—the flush system. Then the sweepers can be free from the stigma of untouchability and assume the dignity of status that is their right as useful members of a casteless and classless society. (145-46)

The poet's speech is a good example of multiculturalism. Multiculturalism not only promotes the value of cultural diversity and social equality but also recognizes equality of rights and privileges. The poet rightly makes people aware of their rights and privileges. Comparatively his thoughts are more relevant, advanced and practical than that of Mahatma Gandhi. As he rightly says caste is a major hurdle in maintaining social integrity, equality, harmony and peace. So let it be destroyed from the social map of India. Furthermore, he states that there is no one-to-one relation between caste and profession, as you can change your profession as you wish. He appeals to the small audience with his enunciation of the reasons of social inequality. After all, caste decides/shapes/spoils human life as birth or the place of birth is less significant than the attached stigma of caste. Obviously, caste divides people and places them in different strata of society. Therefore, caste is one of the major reasons of social inequality. As the poet says that the British-Indian penal code protects and recognizes the equality of rights to all people irrespective of caste, religion or occupation. At the end, he introduces them to the machine (flush system); one of the alternatives that will help them to minimize their work and it will also make them free from the stigma of untouchability. Bakha is delighted by the practical approach of the poet than the spiritual philosophy of Mahatma Gandhi. He returns, enlightened by the poet's idea of the flush system. Mulk Raj Anand appears to believe that rapid industrialization alone would pave the way for a secular situation and he introduces the flush system as a symbol of change. Therefore, Bakha steps out from Hutchinson's religious conversion and Gandhi's spiritual philosophy and finally accepts the poet's idea of machine, a practical solution to the problem of untouchability.

From the beginning, Bakha understands his low and miserable position and feels deeply hurt by the degradation to which he is subjected by the caste Hindus. Throughout the day, insult and humiliation make him restless. Sometimes he gets irritated and tries to revolt against the dominant culture. But his rebelliousness looks ineffective and fruitless, as he knows his limitations at the societal level. Therefore, throughout the novel, Mulk Raj Anand exposes the helplessness of the minority cultures that have been deprived and depressed due to different reasons. However, the dominant culture's social control over power structures remains constant in India. By promoting the notions like purity, impurity or pollution, the dominant culture exploits the minority cultures and deprives them of their social, cultural, economic and political rights. The caste system generates a sense of hatred and enmity among different castes. Bakha, a protagonist of the novel, burns from within throughout the day and finally consoles himself, because he knows that all social problems are deep rooted in Indian caste system that deprives all minority cultures of their basic rights. By depicting the social reality of Indian society, Mulk Raj Anand perhaps wants to reveal that the rift between dominant and subordinate/minority cultures remains a curse to Hindu society. Therefore, at present, Indian Constitution, an important document of multiculturalism is only a source of comfort to the minority cultures.

3

Multiculturalism in *Train to Pakistan*

Train to Pakistan, originally published as *Mano Majra*, portrays the life at the frontier between India and Pakistan that had become the scene of rioting, violence, brutality, cruelty and bloodshed during the partition period in Indian history. The communal synchronization and harmony between the Muslims and the Sikhs, existing for centuries, was shattered by a series of tragic events. The novel presents the tragic tale of the partition period in Indian history. The partition was a political pronouncement, which had caused miseries and sufferings to the people from diverse communities and cultures, particularly the Sikhs, Hindus and Muslims. It had devalued humanistic values and principles and created a sense of hatred, antagonism and hostility among different communities and cultures. This is an analysis of *Train to Pakistan* from the socio-political perspective of multiculturalism. First we look at the history of partition, a necessary background to the analysis of the novel.

August 15, 1947 was a very significant day for the Muslims, Hindus, Sikhs and many others in India. The partition of India, which happened along with the political freedom of the day, was not only a geo-political division of the country into two parts, but it was also a division of religions, cultures, languages, customs, heritage and a lot more. The decision of imprudent and selfish politicians to divide the country on religious grounds had far-reaching consequences on the inhabitants of India. The partition was an outcome of communal politics, the seeds of which were sown in the late 19th century. During the century, British gained full political control over India. They wanted to make the Muslims their allies in order to counter the probable threat of the Hindu educated class. The British also feared a potential threat from the Muslims, since the Muslims were the former rulers of the subcontinent and ruled India for over 300 years under the Mughal Empire. In order to win them over to their side, the British helped and supported the All-India Muslim League. They instilled the notion of separatism in Muslims and gave them separate electorates in the local government of British India.

Though the British followed the policy of divide and rule, their communal politics was organized. During the first decade of the 20th century, the Muslim League and the Indian National Congress formed a collective front against the British rule. But in the 1937 elections, Muslim League received a set back. So the Indian National Congress kept the Muslim League away from the mainstream freedom movement, which led to the League's demand for a separate homeland for Indian Muslims. Gradually, the Muslim League started spreading its roots throughout the continent. In this connection S.R. Chakravarty and M. Hussain (1998: 18) say: "The emergence of the League in Punjab as a strong force had disturbed communal harmony. The Hindus, Muslims and Sikhs had been living as good neighbors, till the spread of the Muslim League in Punjab.... The growing communalism helped the Muslim League's campaign for partition. And during the course of the holocaust there had been widespread violation of common human rights, violence against women, communal riot, looting of properties and arson. People's behavior changed due to partition".

Therefore, the Muslim League's demand for separate homeland created a deep rift between Hindus and Muslims.

However, the Muslim leader, Mohammed Ali Jinnah, felt that the Hindus, by dominating the Indian National Congress, were beginning to dictate terms and indulging in arbitrary decision-making in British India. So in 1940, the All-India

Muslim League declared its desire for a separate state. After League's demand for a separate state, Hindus felt uncomfortable and their good relations started deteriorating. Meanwhile, there was brutal violence spread in some parts of the subcontinent. Finally, the British and Indian leaders such as Nehru, Patel and others decided that the only solution to the conflict was a partition of the country. Lord Mountbatten, the last Viceroy of India, confirmed the possibility of transferring power to two governments, not one. Keeping this in mind, he pressed and finally persuaded the Congress to accept the idea of dividing India. In fact, Mahatma Gandhi did not welcome this idea of division along the lines of religion. The Viceroy made the announcement of partition and declared the boundaries of the two nations—India and Pakistan.

Thus, Pakistan founded its new Islamic Republic on August 14, 1947, whereas in the midnight of the next day, i.e. August 15, 1947, India celebrated its political freedom. For Indians, the partition was a logical outcome of Britain's policy of divide and rule, but for Pakistan it was the outcome of the struggle of Muslims to have their separate identity recognized by both the British and the Indian nationalist movement. However, the partition, without settling any problem, unnecessarily heightened each other's enmity and hostility. From the time of the birth of the two nations, communal riots flared up from distant villages to cities. In fact, the tragedy of partition had given birth to a number of problems, which are still burning in the political and social spheres of both the countries. It is said that partition was a need of the time but nobody considered its adverse impact on the masses. Some political leaders were very much eager to see the division of the country, because they wanted to satisfy their political thirst to be a first Prime Minister of the nations formed. They did not consider the emotional, cultural, religious and social attachment maintained by the people of different communities. Partition did not merely divide a nation, but many families also got divided; thousands of people were dislocated, and many lost their belongings and everything. In other words, it was the division of a whole composite and synergetic civilization and culture of a rich country. Therefore, partition is not only a tragedy of one group or a nation but also a tragedy of the whole 'Hindustan', previously known as a composite and amalgamated entity having a large space on the map of the world.

In *Train to Pakistan*, Khushwant Singh tries to unfurl the history of India's partition and its horrifying consequences at all levels—religious, cultural, social and political. As a literary artist, Khushwant Singh deals with many issues related to politics, religion, caste, culture and identity. The aim of this chapter is to show how Khushwant Singh delineates the impact of partition on a multicultural society that was known for peaceful coexistence of various communities, cultures and religions. The sociological perspective adopted here for a theoretical framework underlines the value of cultural pluralism, non-discrimination, respect to socio-cultural diversity, heterogeneity, recognition of differences and equality, harmonious coexistence, religious tolerance and value of egalitarian society. For the sake of interpretative convenience, the novel is analyzed along two separate lines: the first line involves a pre-partition period in which the above-mentioned principles of multiculturalism are more or less reflected in the novel. In the pre-partition Punjab, all the residents of Mano Majra, irrespective of their caste, religion, creed and culture, had tacitly acknowledged and adopted multiculturalism as a policy framework. The second line focuses on the post-partition period in the novel, which brings socio-cultural disharmony, communal hatred, social unrest, cultural dislocation, disrespect, antipathy, enmity, discrimination, displacement, disintegration, doubt, intolerance and failure of human values. It also deals with the rise of destructive communal and religious identities, which damaged the socio-cultural harmony and peaceful coexistence of the Mano Majra residents. The second line of analysis, in short, clearly shows how the principles of multiculturalism have been violated in the post-partition period.

Train to Pakistan presents Mano Majra, a border village of Punjab, with its religious, cultural, and ethnic characteristics.

Although of diverse backgrounds, the people of the village had been residing together with much respect and love for one another. Their peaceful coexistence nurtured human values like love, trust and respect in the public domain. In the pre-partition period, Sikhs, Hindus, and Muslims in Mano Majra made a positive contribution to solidify a cultural mosaic in Punjab. Different cultural and religious groups were free to define their own ways of life. They could enjoy their religious, cultural and linguistic practices and customary ways. They respected each other's religion and culture and encouraged the differences in terms of food habits, life styles, beliefs and different cultural and religious practices. In a sense, all communities and cultures were quite accommodative and open to accept the fact of social diversity, one of the principles of multiculturalism.

Unfortunately, partition along religious lines cracks the solidarity and integrity of the village. A culture of content turns to a culture of discontent, hatred and violence. P.K Singh (2005: 40) has effectively summarized the sudden and unexpected turn of emotions: "Anger alternates affection. Love alternates with hate and desire alternates with greed. The traditional, social and religious stratification is overridden by the communal feelings." It seems that in his novel Khushwant Singh wants to present Mano Majra as a microcosm of pre-partition India, where human beings could establish relationships irrespective of their religious and cultural differences.

The novel opens with a depiction of the multicultural setting of Mano Majra. The occupational and religious diversity of its inhabitants is reflected in the following extract:

> Mano Majra is a tiny place. It has only three brick buildings, one of which is the home of the moneylender Lala Ram Lal. The other two are the Sikh temple and the mosque. The three brick buildings enclose a triangular common with a large people tree in the middle. The rest of the village is a cluster of flat-roofed mud huts and low-walled courtyards, which front on narrow lanes that radiate from the center.... At the

> western end of the village there is a pond ringed round by keeker trees. There are only about seventy families in Mano Majra, and Lala Ram Lal's is the only Hindu family. The others are Sikhs or Muslims, about equal in number. The Sikhs own all the land around the village; the Muslims are tenants and share the tilling with the owners. There are few families of sweepers whose religion is uncertain. (10)

The extract reveals the multicultural face of the village, Mano Majra. The Sikhs, Hindus and Muslims have been living side by side with a range of varying cultures, ideals and customs. They call each other brothers. In fact, there is no inequality and disparity between majority and minority. This is how they value the principles of multiculturalism. There are a few families of sweepers whose religion is uncertain. Sometimes "they visit the Sikh temple, too" (10). It means without any communal and religious clashes, the Mano Majrans have lived joyfully. Indeed, in their own unpolished ways they discuss religious and cultural issues, but the debates, while pointing up differences, often lead to conclusions which underscore the need for peaceful coexistence rather than rude compartmentalization. Without any preconceived notions of cultural superiority or inferiority, they simply acknowledge socio-cultural diversity as an integral part of their life. Their positive approach to socio-cultural diversity helps them to extend their sympathies to others, deepen their self-knowledge and enrich their way of life. They not only recognize the fact of socio-cultural diversity, but voluntarily respect 'differences'. They respect differences in terms of culture, religion, ideology, ways of thinking, feeling, lifestyle, dress codes, habits and so on. The socio-cultural diversity encourages a healthy competition between them.

For years, these communities in the village have shared and balanced their languages, beliefs, ideals, religions, cultures and attitudes and gained for themselves a peaceful and harmonious life. Their harmonious social coexistence is a real illustration of a slogan of multiculturalism, i.e. 'Living together separately.' Khushwant Singh depicts this kind of a socio-religious unity in diversity. It seems to promote the values of an egalitarian society, one of the ideals of multiculturalism. Consider these lines which underline the tolerance of the Mano Majrans:

> This is a three-foot slab of sandstone that stands upright under a keeker tree beside the pond. It is the local deity, the deo to which all the villagers—Hindu, Sikh, Muslim or pseudo-Christian—repair secretly whenever they are in special need of blessing. (10-11)

The local deity or deo symbolizes Mano Majra's socio-religious unity and communal harmony. With the help of this example, Khushwant Singh speaks not only of the value of religious diversity but also the fusion of multiple religious ideologies under the single umbrella term 'deo'. This kind of socio-religious unity in diversity shows the presence of multiculturalism in pre-partition Punjab. It is said that religious fanaticism divides people into different groups, but this local deity becomes a binding force of religious rationalization and social cohesion of Mano Majra. After all, each religion is an institution that preaches to its followers how to nurture the universal principles of humanity, brotherhood, equality, respect, tolerance, love and peace. Therefore, all the villagers of Mano Majra, irrespective of their caste, community and culture, worship this local deity without disturbing their own religious identity. However, by glorifying the presence of a local deity, Khushwant Singh also promotes the value of monotheism, a central faith of Sikhism. As we know, religion occupies an important place in the history of civilization and philosophy, and it is believed to give meaning and purpose to human life. It satisfies man's longing for peace and salvation. Therefore, religious diversity in Mano Majra creates no problem at social level. In spite of their belief in a common deity, they understand each other's distinctive beliefs and religious practices.

Being a Sikh, Khushwant Singh glorifies Sikhism which he feels is more accommodative and receptive than other religions. Guru Nanak, the founder of Sikhism, rejected socio-religious hegemony and socio-economic divisions of Hindu Brahmanical society. Sikhism, the third largest religion in India, was born out of the good intention of bringing together the best of Hinduism and Islam. It recognizes God as the only creator, sustainer and destroyer of the universe. So it rejects all rituals and practices and promotes the value of human life based on love, respect, trust and mutual understanding. Guru Nanak challenged the programme of dividing people into classes, castes and communities. He believed that all men of different cultures and religions were equally worthy of respect and love. Indirectly Sikhism rejects all distinctions of caste, creed, and gender and believes in a casteless egalitarian society that guarantees equal rights to all people. Therefore, religious principles of Sikhism lie very close to the tenets of multiculturalism. It is said that Sikhism is quite modern, open and rational and it promotes the principle of equality. The local deity in Mano Majra stands for its inhabitants' cohesiveness and religious unity. Khushwant Singh depicts various scenes related to religious diversity and cultural plurality of Mano Majra. The peaceful coexistence of the Sikhs and Muslims in the novel is suggestive of his idea of an egalitarian society. Without any friction or conflict, both communities respect each other's culture and religion. This kind of respect and tolerance is a clear sign of the healthy existence of a multicultural society. Multiculturalism acknowledges the freedom of all members of society which helps them to preserve, enhance and share their religious and cultural heritage. In some multicultural societies, religious diversity and cultural plurality often lead to communal clashes, but in Mano Majra, especially Sikhs and Muslims consider each other as brothers.

Multiculturalism does not differentiate between the majority and the minority on the basis of numerical strength. It advocates and celebrates differences in terms of religion, culture, ideology and different ways of life. In Mano Majra, Muslims are in minority but they feel comfortable and secure in the village. The religious security and preference they enjoy are revealed in these words:

> The mullah at the mosque knows that it is time for Morning Prayer. He has a quick wash, stands facing

> west towards Mecca and with his fingers in his ears cries in long sonorous notes, "Allah-ho-Akbar". The priest at the Sikh temple lies in bed till the mullah has called. Then he gets up, draws a bucket of water from the well in the temple courtyard, pours it over himself, and intones his prayer in monotonous singsong to the sound of splashing water. (12-13)

This extract is a good example of multiculturalism. Instead of cultural clashes and religious intolerance, Sikhs and Muslims engage in their religious practices without weakening the social health of Mano Majra. As we know religion and culture influence each other at various levels. Religion shapes a culture's system of belief and practices, whereas culture transmits religious values and beliefs from one generation to another for the escalation of social health. Therefore, we, as social animals, cannot separate religion and culture, which are the determinant factors for shaping human society. In the above extract, the Muslim mullah and the Sikh priest are the representatives of different religions who can perform their religious duties without feeling of religious jealousy and communal hatred. Thus, the Mullah's long sonorous note "Allah-ho-Akbar" is a reminder for the Sikh priest to 'be ready' for his prayer. He says his faithful prayer "by shouting at the top of his voice, *God is great*" (14). This kind of religious understanding and tolerance definitely promotes the value of religious unity in diversity. The Mullah's sonorous note of "Allah-ho-Akbar" and the Sikh priest's monotonous "singsong" show their different ways of prayer, but their religious diversity is not harmful to the rest of the society. After all, every religion preaches universal values of equality, love, respect, devotion and peace. Here unity in religious diversity is considered to be a positive step towards promoting the principles of multiculturalism, which support nature's basic law of equality.

Khushwant Singh has also dealt with the different modes of worship of the Sikhs and Muslims in Mano Majra, which underlines the way each group maintains its religious identity:

> In the mosque, a dozen men stood in two rows silently going through their genuflections. In the gurudwara, Meet Singh sitting beside the book which was folded up in muslin on a cot, was recited the evening prayer. Five or six men and women sat in a semi-circle around a hurricane lantern and listened to him. (59)

In Islam, women are not allowed in the mosque for reciting prayers, whereas in Sikhism men and women both are sitting together in a semi-circle for prayer. Standing in a 'row' and sitting in a 'semi-circle' indicate differences in modes of religious worship. Compared to Sikhism, Islam is more conservative, but its conservatism does not make the Sikhs critical. Differences in religious practices are vividly narrated. The narration illustrates the fact that no religion in Mano Majra has an inferior status and the follower of each religion has a sense of equality in religious affairs. Further, as the extract suggests, multiculturalism doesn't rest only on a single principle of equality but it promotes other human values like tolerance, love and respect. Thus, multiculturalism is not only an ideological theory, but it has concrete expressions in social life.

The openness and the readiness to acknowledge and accept the 'other' is a character trait of most of the inhabitants of Mano Majra. Assertion of one's own religious belief thus finds expression in accommodating the 'other'. Consider, e.g. how Meet Singh welcomes the stranger, Iqbal, when the latter seeks accommodation in the gurudwara:

> "Sat Sri Akal."
>
> "Sat Sri Akal."
>
> "Can I stay for two or three days?"
>
> "This is gurudwara, the Guru's house-anyone may stay her.... Put your luggage in that room and make yourself comfortable. Will you have something to eat?" (47)

The interaction between Meet Singh and Iqbal shows religious openness and belief of the Sikhs in cultural plurality. As a religion, Sikhism preaches humanism and encourages community service. Meet Singh always respects and cares for

Iqbal. He enquires: "Iqbal Singhji, have you gone to bed without food? Would you like some spinach? I have also curd and buttermilk" (59). Meet Singh's humanitarian care speaks a lot about his religion, a religion of humanity.

The multiculturalism reflected in the opening part of the novel is a positive step towards fostering the value of social integrity and peace. In brief, Meet Singh's way of greeting, polite language, etiquette, respect to the Sikh scriptures and above all his hospitality reveal the multidimensionality of the Sikh culture, which essentially promotes humanism, egalitarianism, socio-religious liberalism and multicultural harmony. Therefore, the harmonious coexistence mirrored in the above extract is considered to be a positive sign of multiculturalism.

The conversation between Meet Singh and Iqbal reveal the former's practical sense and the latter's proclivity for rhetoric. Iqbal, having been abroad, has a fascination for the western way of life, but is unable to acknowledge the Christians' freedom to preach religion. He seeks material comfort but Meet Singh stands for values:

> Everyone is welcome to his religion. Here next door is a Muslim mosque. When I pray to my Guru, uncle Imam Baksh calls to Allah. How many religions do they have in Europe? (49)

Iqbal, at the same time, praises the monotheism of Europe. He is oblivious of the hegemonic attitude of monotheistic European religion to the other religions:

> They are all Christians of one kind or another. They do not quarrel about their religions as we do here. They do not really bother very much about religion. (49)

This obviously, shows that Christianity is the only religion in European countries, which creates no wave of quarrel and conflict among different ethnic groups. Because they are monotheistic Christians enjoy peaceful coexistence without any friction and conflict. Perhaps, Khushwant Singh wants to compare these two religions, i.e. Sikhism and Christianity, on the basis of their common belief in the concept of 'monotheism'. But in a multireligious and multicultural India, 'monotheism' is not a proper step to envelope all social problems related to caste, culture, gender, equality and human rights. Therefore, multiculturalism is a better option, which encompasses all the above-mentioned aspects. As a matter of fact, India is a multireligious and multicultural country, where people believe in different 'avatars' of God and perform different religious practices. So it is not easy to make them stand together under the single concept of 'monotheism'. Khushwant Singh's purpose here is to convey the message that no society, whether monotheistic or polytheistic, can boast of social harmony if its religion(s) fails to teach the values of communal harmony, religious diversity and cultural plurality.

By portraying different scenes of communal harmony and religious diversity, Khushwant Singh wants to project the idea of secularism which was strongly promoted by Mahatma Gandhi and supported by other social reformers in pre-partition India. Surprisingly, it is a Muslim in the novel who praises Mahatma Gandhi's idea of secularism and religious harmony:

> "If we have no faith in God then we are like animals," said the Muslim gravely. All the world respects a religious man. Look at Gandhi! I hear he reads the Koran Sharif and the Unjeel along his Vedas and Shastras. People sing his praise in the four corners of the earth. I have seen a picture in a newspaper of Gandhi's prayer meeting. It showed a lot of white men and women sitting cross-legged. One white girl had her eyes shut. They said she was the Big Lord's daughter. You see, Meet Singh, even the English respect a man of religion. (63)

The Muslim speaker recognizes the importance of godly presence, religion and culture in human society. By making him quote Mahatma Gandhi's example of secularism, Khushwant Singh tries to link up multiculturalism with secularism and draw the conclusion that, principally, both 'isms' are the same. Secularism promotes the equality of all religions, without special favor to any particular one. For Khushwant Singh, secularism means the freedom to practice one's religion in one's own house. Outside the house, all religions are equal but different in practice. It obviously means that, ideally, secularism in India promotes the principles of multiculturalism. Khushwant Singh's introduction of the Gandhian Muslim is an attempt to assert the value of multiculturalism in India. He seems to assert the idea that Mahatma Gandhi's secularism is one of the versions of Indian multiculturalism, which encompasses religious and cultural tolerance and promotes the value of equality. It is, therefore, assumed that secularism in India is supposed to mean western multiculturalism which is now becoming a working policy in the multicultural societies. In a multireligious and multicultural country like India, there can be no peace without tolerance and respect to different religions and cultures. If we fail to accept the challenge of secularism and multiculturalism, definitely there would be a threat of disharmony and division on the basis of community and religious fanaticism. Khushwant Singh highlights this point in *Train to Pakistan*.

Though language and culture are interrelated, we do not always find a one-to-one correspondence between them. As we know language is a symbolic entity, but it doesn't carry only a symbolic meaning; it also signals the cultural behavior of the speaker, i.e. his cultural identity. So the speaker's language not only reflects his way of thinking and feeling but also his cultural identity. After all, language is one of the most sensitive instruments used for maintaining good human relations. Claire Kramsch (1998: 77) points out: "Although there is no one-to-one relationship between anyone's language and his or her cultural identity, language is the most sensitive indicator of the relationship between an individual and a given social group. Any harmony or disharmony between the two is registered on his most sensitive of the Richter Scales."

By pointing up the relationship between language and culture, here, we analyze some conversational exchanges, which reflect the speakers' cultural and religious identities having a positive sense of harmony, respect, affection, hospitality and love. The Sikhs and Muslims greet Iqbal in the

Gurudwara and discuss things with him. The way they use language reflects their affinity, respect and love for each other:

> Then he got up to greet the visitors.
>
> 'Sat Sri Akal, Babu Sahib.'
>
> 'Salaam to you, Babu Sahib.'
>
> They shook hands. Meet Singh did not bother to introduce them. He pushed the air mattress aside to make room on the charpoy for the visitors and sat down on the floor himself.
>
> 'I am ashamed for not having presented myself earlier.' said the Sikh. 'Please forgive me. I have brought some milk for you.'... 'Here, Babuji, drink it before it gets cold.'... 'Yes you drink it as you like, Babuji,' said the Muslim. (60-61)

These conversational exchanges speak a lot about multiculturalism. Every speaker, irrespective of his communal, religious or cultural identity, speaks politely with each other and maintains the principles of multiculturalism. Multiculturalism values dialogues between communities and cultures. It believes that a single dialogue can reduce friction and conflict in a multicultural society. Such a dialogue has already taken place between Meet Singh and Iqbal. The words of greetings like 'Sat Sri Akal' and 'Salaam' in the above extract directly reflect the speakers' religious identity. Without any ill-feeling, they respect and recognize each other's religion, community and culture. Therefore, this kind of relationship encapsulates all human values being recognized by different religions and cultures. The Sikh's apologetic words, 'Please forgive me', indicate his politeness and deep-rooted sense of his culture. Actually he is not a defaulter of any kind, but his utterance reflects his culture. He even offers a tumbler of milk to Iqbal. This again shows his sense of hospitality to the guest who belongs nowhere. Furthermore, the Muslim visitor's friendly insistence to Iqbal on having a glass of milk reveals his culture and a sense of hospitability to the unknown guest. In a sense, every individual is a carrier of his/her culture, which is seen in different forms, may be through language, behavior, attitude and lot of human activities. Therefore, we see how the principles of multiculturalism have been reflected in the above conversational exchanges. After all, utility, implementation and result of any social or political theory depend on the context in which it is used or applied.

To sum up, multiculturalism builds a bridge between different cultures. But bridging the difference presupposes a minimum of balance between the cultures. After all, each culture has its own value and it articulates diverse aspects of good life. So multiculturalism respects differences and ensures equality for culturally and socially diverse groups. This first line of analysis interprets how multiculturalism is a social reality seen in a multicultural village called Mano Majra. The villagers have accepted socio-cultural diversity as a need for maintaining their social health. Irrespective of their caste, religion and culture, they have respected each other, maintaining equality, brotherhood, humanity and love. By promoting the value of religious diversity and cultural equality, they have planted a tree of social integrity, harmony and peace. Their religious tolerance is an effective tonic for their social health. It also supplies the food material for nurturing the values of an egalitarian society. Therefore, multiculturalism reflected in pre-partition Punjab is a good sign of social, religious and cultural equality. It also shows how all kinds of differences should be valued and protected in a positive way that will help people to add different colors and flavors to their lives.

But the second line of analysis focuses on the evil consequences of partition. Though partition is a political decision, taken by the so-called leaders, on the basis of religion, it has disturbed and troubled the peaceful coexistence of masses that are neither acquainted with the British rule nor familiar with any local government. Multiculturalism, a social ideology, gets disturbed with the decision of partition. In fact, the Mano Majrans are quite ignorant about the political leaders' decision. Their ignorance is seen in the following extract. The Sikhs and the Muslims ask Iqbal about partition:

> 'Well, Babuji,' began the Muslim. 'Tell us something. What is happening in the world? What is all this about Pakistan and Hindustan?' We live in this little village and know nothing, the lambardar put in. 'Babuji, tell us, why did the English leave?' (61)

Iqbal is unable to answer their simple questions. The simplicity of their questions shows how they are unaware and ignorant about India's independence and its aftermath. Independence means nothing to them, for their coexistence had known no bondage. But out of curiosity, they just ask Iqbal about the happening in the world. The Muslim's innocent question 'What is all this about Pakistan and Hindustan?' speaks a lot about their innocence and ignorance. Actually ordinary people are not acquainted with the communal distinction between Pakistan and Hindustan; they simply live their peaceful life. For them "independence meant little or nothing" (61). As a fact, they have already cultivated and fostered the principles of multiculturalism. Now they are quite worried about partition, which has made them culturally and socially separate. They are less acquainted with a 'brutish rule' of the British who had been ruling the nation for decades. In this regard, S.P. Swain (1999: 85-86) says: "Mano Majrans are unaware of the political situation of the country. They even do not know that British have left India and that India has been partitioned and is ruled now by the popular congress ministry."

Iqbal tries to make them grasp the meaning of political freedom. He says: "Do you want to remain slaves all your lives?" (62). But nobody gives any answer to his question. After a long silence, the Lambardar answers: "freedom must be a good thing. But what will we get out of it? Educated people like you, Babu Sahib, will get the jobs the English had" (62). The Lambardar's answer reveals a rift between the educated and uneducated people. He believes that the educated are the only beneficiaries of independence while other illiterate peasants always remain slaves. One of the Muslims also supports the Lambardar and states: "We were slaves of the English, now we will be slaves of the educated Indians—or the

Pakistani" (62). It means, for them slavery is common. The only difference is that how much and in what way the native colonizers' go on exploiting them. For ordinary masses, partition brings nothing, neither freedom nor happiness. Khushwant Singh tries to bring in social realism and pragmatism. In pre-independence India, educated people have enjoyed more privileges and civil rights than the uneducated people, because of their fascination for British culture and education. But the minority cultures, which were deprived of education, remained speechless. As a result, their slavish mindset persisted. This shows how partition has made no positive effect on the lives of ordinary people. Therefore, they prefer to maintain and preserve their age-old communal harmony, love, mutual understanding, social peace, respect and recognition of each other's cultural and religious differences. Unfortunately, partition has made their lives more insecure and anxious.

One cannot blame the Mano Majrans for their ignorance of the effects of partition. Living on the fringes of the country, like a marginalized group, they did not receive much attention from either the British or the natives. They were least affected by the westernization of India and as long as they remained unaware of it, there was peace and harmony. The question is, did political freedom add to Indian multiculturalism, and the answer is not always an emphatic 'yes'.

Iqbal's anti-colonial attitude is revealed in his words: "if you want freedom to mean something for you—the peasants and workers—you have to get together and fight" (62). But his words have no effect on the Lambardar and other villagers, because they are quite sure and definite about the social reality. As the Lambardar says: "The winds of destruction are blowing across the land. All we hear is kill, kill. The only ones who enjoy freedom are thieves, robbers and cut-throats" (64). The Lambardar's remark suggests that partition brings happiness and freedom only to those who are thieves, robbers and cut-throats. The weak and illiterate minority groups always remain away from the so-called 'fruits' of partition. Therefore, ordinary people of different communities and religions try to maintain their socio-cultural harmony and religious diversity. But the blow of partition threatens their attempt to safeguard socio-cultural harmony and religious diversity.

Sadly, partition creates waves of communal hatred and disharmony in different parts of the country. In fact, common people are not happy with the political decision of partition which permanently dislocate and displace them from their soil and socio-cultural harmony. Therefore, partition is not a welcome idea to the masses that are the sufferers and the victims of its evil consequences. Before partition, there existed peace, coexistence and social harmony in Mano Majra. But partition comes with socio-cultural disharmony, communal jealousy, sense of insecurity and a lot of other things which spoil and ruin the lives of thousands of Muslims, Sikhs and Hindus. Therefore, the tragedy of partition creates a number of problems in Mano Majra. In this context, Chirantan Kulshrestha (1977: 127) says: "The novel does not offer to tell a story: its chief protagonist is not a particular person, but a village. The method is thus essentially sociological: Khushwant Singh sees in the border village, Mano Majra, a microcosm of the communal temper of the country in the days following the partition. The peaceful of village is disturbed when the communal virus infects the people. Old roots are destroyed and revenge becomes the order of day".

The harmonious and peaceful life of Mano Majra is suddenly disturbed by the arrival of a ghostly train from Pakistan which is loaded with the dead bodies of Sikhs. The train looks something unusual and different, "there are no lights on the train, the engine did not whistle, it is like a ghost train" (163). The train brings not only the dead bodies of Sikhs but also commotion, turmoil, communal hatred and jealousy. For centuries, the Sikhs and Muslims have lived together in Mano Majra with great quietude. But partition has changed the whole scene. The head constable's visit to the village divides "Mano Majra into two halves as neatly as a knife cuts through a part of butter" (141). The stormy rumors of atrocities committed by the Sikhs on Muslims and the Muslims on Sikhs spread all over the country. As a result, people from both the communities feel suspicious of each other's religious and cultural identities. The social peace, tranquility and harmony of Mano Majra get disrupted due to the arrival of the ghostly train. For the first time, the Sikhs and Muslims see an unusual train, a symbol of destruction and obliteration. Though the Sikhs in the village are in majority; they start distrusting their Muslim brothers. Some of them even say: "never trust a Musalman" (141). The Sikhs sit in a circle around a hurricane lantern, some of them on a charpoy and others on the floor. One of the younger men speaks: "We have looked upon the Muslims as our brothers and sisters. Why should they send somebody to spy on us?" (143). The arrival of the ghostly train has created a tense atmosphere in Mano Majra. Their age-old relations become murky and gloomy. In a sense, the train comes with a message of prospective, undying enmity and hostility between the two communities. As a result, the Sikhs and Muslims have started suspecting each other's communal, religious and cultural identities. Rumors of communal riots, slaughter, massacre and butchery spread all over the country.

Though communal and cultural respect is replaced by enmity, hostility and suspicion, Mano Majra remains peaceful and free from any communal frenzy, because of people's emotional involvement with each other irrespective of their caste, community, religion and culture. As Twinkle B. Manavar (1998: 31) says: "Partition touched Mano Majra at both levels—at the community level and at the individual level. At the community level it affects very badly the Hindus, Muslims and Sikhs. The dark clouds of suspicion and fear arise among the Sikhs and Muslims, who have lived together for centuries. Yet feelings of brotherliness have not disappeared, and they meet for consultation in a scene that is both intensely humane and touching".

Before long, sadly, the impact of partition begins to be felt. Yet there is a conscious and intelligent attempt on the part of the local religious leaders to maintain the harmony and synchronization of Mano Majra intact. They hear the shocking news of communal riots in Pakistan. They "had heard of mosques being desecrated by the slaughter of pigs on the premises, and of copies of the holy Koran being torn up by infidels" (141). The Muslims in Mano Majra feel insecure and anxious, therefore Imam Baksh, a Muslim mullah, goes with his fellow beings to meet Sikh leaders:

> 'Well, brothers, what is your decision about us?' he asked quietly.
>
> There was an awkward silence. Everyone looked at the lambardar.
>
> 'Why ask us?' answered the lambardar. 'This is your village as much as ours.'
>
> You have heard what is being said! All the neighboring villages have been evacuated. Only we are left. If you want us to go too, we will go.'
>
> Meet Singh began to sniff.... One of the younger men spoke.
>
> 'It is like this, Uncle Imam Baksh. As long as we are here nobody will dare to touch you. We die first and then you can look after yourself.' ...Imam Baksh wiped a tear from his eyes and blew his nose on the hem of his shirt.' (146-47)

This indeed is a touching scene. It suggests how the human emotion of love can transcend all barriers of selfishness and unconcern. Without any feeling of communal hatred and enmity, both the Sikhs and the Muslims have enjoyed their own ways of life. But the storm of partition ruptures and scatters their age-old relations. Numerically, the Sikhs are in a majority, whereas the Muslims are in a minority. Before partition, there was no social friction or conflict between the two communities on the basis of their numerical strength—majority and minority. Both the communities have maintained their healthy relations. But partition fractures their socio-cultural, socio-religious and socio-communal harmony.

Imam Baksh's words in the above extract create an awkward silence in their meeting. But both the communities try to reassert their emotional integrity, attachment, respect and tolerance to each other. Thus the exchange of words between

Sikhs and Muslims reveals their age-old cultural, religious and social integrity. Even the Lambardar's words of support speak a lot about the Sikh-Muslim unity in the village which is to be threatened due to the partition. His statement, 'this is your village as much as ours', reveals Mano Majra's social integrity and communal harmony. Moreover, Lambardar says: "you are our brothers. As far as we are concerned, you and your children and your grand children can live here as long as you like" (147). His encouraging words carry valuable messages that are quite close to the theory of multiculturalism.

One of the younger men gives moral support to Imam Baksh and promises him not to be worried about any danger. The promising words of the young man 'nobody will dare to touch you', highlight Sikh-Muslim unity in the village. But moment-by-moment their unity is breaking. After his discussion with his Sikh brothers, Imam Baksh is overcome with emotion. His tears signify his community's deep attachment to and emotional involvement with his Sikh brothers. Perhaps the thoughts of their pre-partition life are welling up in his mind. During the pre-partition period, they maintained communal harmony, brotherhood and equality within the village. But their peaceful coexistence is challenged not so much by the political or social implications of partition as by the selfish activities of a few brutish men.

True, the bond of fraternal feelings existing between Sikhs and Muslims in Mano Majra is devastated by the regrettable decision of partition. In fact, nobody likes the political decision of partition taken by the so-called politicians on the basis of religion. The sub-inspector's bitter comment shows his animosity against the political leaders who have taken the political decision of partition:

> What do the Gandhi-caps in Delhi know about the Punjab? What is happening on the other side in Pakistan does not matter to them. They have not lost their homes and belongings; they haven't had their mothers, wives, sisters and daughters raped and murdered in the streets. (31)

This extract exemplifies how the political leaders take important decisions in Delhi without bearing in mind its evil consequences and effects on the masses. It is a tragedy of the masses that they have to be the worst sufferers of the decision of partition. It is true that neither political leaders nor policy makers have lost their homes and belongings. But the masses, the real custodians of human values, continuously suffer and burn in the flames of communal frenzy and agitation. Therefore, the sub-inspector's bitter comment on the political leaders' decision discloses the distance between the political leaders and the unspeaking masses. Moreover, his bitter comment also reveals how the partition has not only spoiled the peaceful lives of the masses but also challenged the communal and social harmony of Mano Majra. As we know, in the field of politics, the powerful lobby takes political decisions which many times, goes against the masses. If we see the history of any partition, generally we find how the masses get victimized in the form of dislocation and displacement. But the so-called decision makers always remain safe from any communal frenzy or displacement. The partition of India is no exception.

Obviously, thousands of innocent people of Mano Majra have to become the victims of partition. Yet, Imam Baksh, a representative of the Muslim community, is not ready to leave the place. He poignantly expresses the Muslims' deep sense of involvement with and attachment to the Sikhs who are now becoming the custodians of the village:

> What have we done with Pakistan? We were born here. So were our ancestors. We have lived amongst you as brothers. Imam Baksh broke down. Meet Singh clasped him in his arms and began to sob. Several of the people started crying quietly and blowing their noses. (147)

The Imam's words imply the value of multiculturalism. What is unbearable to him is the cultural dislocation rather than the geographical dislodging. Moving on to an alien land with which he has no emotional commitment but is a punishment. The Imam also underlines the fact that the source of harmony does not lie in the physical proximity of a group of people belonging to the same religion/community. The Muslim environment in Pakistan is an anathema to the Imam and his people. This is because they have forged strong human and cultural bonds in Mano Majra which have sustained them for centuries. They can maintain their cultural identity and individuality only in the border village. The Muslims of Mano Majra are not ready to fracture their age-old harmony, synchronization and social cohesion. Every word of the Imam signals Muslim-Sikh emotional integrity and close involvement with each other. In a sense, their emotional integrity is a sign of respect and tolerance to each other's religion and culture. But partition makes them leave the place with tears in their eyes.

The response to the Imam's question in the passage quoted above is Meet Singh's tears. Both these leaders share and recognize the value of cultural differences and hence they can feel the senselessness of a geo-political partition. The common people also share the views of these two local religious leaders. Certainly, there have been lines of demarcation in Mano Majra, but such lines of separation only added to its inhabitants' capability to cut across social and religious lines. They have their own religions but they respect each other's religiosity. If they know the differences, they use the knowledge to assert the other's right to retain his/her own identity. That the Sikhs' desire cultural diversity in Mano Majra is evident from these words of the Lambardar:

> It is for your own safety that I advise you to take shelter in the camp for a few days, and then you come back. As far as we are concerned, he repeated warmly, "if you decide to stay on, you are most welcome to do so. We will defend you with our lives". (148)

It is to be remembered that the Sikh community is in a state of dilemma. Their own people have come to the village as refugees from Pakistan. The protection of these refugees, driven out by the Muslims in Pakistan, is in the hands of the Sikhs. At the same time, they have to protect a group of local Muslim refugees whom they have known for centuries. As the Lambardar promises his Muslim brothers: "you lock your houses with your belongings. We will look after your cattle till you come back" (148). It is true that the Lambardar is fairly helpless, but his promising words to Muslim brothers indicate his deep involvement with them. But at last his promising words become futile because of a swelling flow of the Sikh refugees from Pakistan.

Soon there occurs a clash of ideas between the extremist group on the one hand and Meet Singh and the Lambardar on the other. As the narrator says: "Group loyalty was above reason" (145). Meet Singh is not interested in knowing what is happening to the Muslims at the other parts of India and Pakistan. His sole concern, at the moment, is Mano Majra, his own real world. He is aware of the suffering and pain of the Sikhs in Pakistan. But his interrogation of the militant Sikh youths is revealing: "I was only talking of Mano Majra. What have our tenants done?" (144). The Lambardar is also aware of the stupidity of the vengeance that the youths talk about. He makes an attempt to control the situation by lowering his voice: "This is no time to lose tempers. Nobody here wants to kill anyone" (145). He tells one of them: "You are a hot-headed one...we say one thing and you drag the talk to something else" (145). He can talk more sensibly and in accommodative terms. He wants to receive the Sikh refugees from Pakistan but not at the cost of Mano Majra Muslims' lives: "Are we going to tell them (the Sikh refugees): 'do not come to this village?' And if they do come, will we let them wreak vengeance on our tenants?" (145). Surprisingly, the multicultural view of Meet Singh and the Lambardar was happily shared by the local masses, too. Consider, for example, these lines: "The peasants thought about their (refugees') problem...emphatically not" (145). In this respect, K.K. Sharma (1984: 77) says: "They (Sikhs) were in terrible dilemma. They could not refuse shelter to the homeless Sikhs driven away from Pakistan, and they could not let their Muslim tenants run away from their village. Their age-old love for their fellow Muslims remained unshaken against heavy odds, and their anger turned into bewilderment. They were concerned about the safety of the Muslims. This confirmed Mano Majra as the fine example of communal harmony and integration".

However, the Muslims themselves understand the necessity to leave for Pakistan. Even their departure is a self-less act. Imam Baksh says solemnly: "if we have to go, we'd better pack up our bedding and belongings" (148). They have to uproot themselves from Mano Majra, their homeland, and start life anew in an alien land. They don't seem to believe that they would be able to 'settle' down in Pakistan by forging new cultural ties. Yet they have to leave. But once again the Sikhs and the Muslims part their ways in peace, even as the vultures of intolerance and communalism hover around. The two groups, however, have grown above the base and mean ways of this world. The Lambardar gets up, embraces Imam Baksh and starts crying loudly. They part in love acknowledging each other's helplessness:

> Sikh and Muslim villagers fell into each other's arms and wept like children. Imam Baksh gently got out of the Lambardar's embrace. 'There is no need to cry', he said between sobs. This is the way of the world. (149)

This pathetic scene points up how partition gives birth to miseries, sufferings and develops a sense of cultural rootlessness among the people. The words like weeping, crying, sobbing and embracing denote the pathetic condition of the Sikhs and the Muslims who are unable to control their feelings of separation. Imam Baksh concludes the informal meeting by making the statement: 'This is the way of the world'. Imam Baksh and his companions leave the meeting in tears. When he goes back to his house, he wakes up his lovable daughter, Nooran, and says: "Nooro, Nooro...get up and pack. We have to go away tomorrow morning" (149). In her sleep, Nooran asks her father: "Go away? Where?" (149). But the helpless father knows nothing about the new place, where they are supposed to go. Therefore, he replies: "I don't know... Pakistan!" (149). On one hand, this conversational exchange shows Muslims' deep involvement with the Sikhs and on the other, their ignorance about their 'mysterious' and 'unknown' future.

However, the above passage gives adequate information about the helplessness of the Sikhs and the Muslims who have been torn between different forces like politics, caste, community, religion and culture. Until the partition, both communities had adopted a slogan of multiculturalism, i.e. 'living together separately'. But the partition really separates them, at least physically.

Significantly, even at the moment of partition hope rules their minds. Indeed partition brings misery, distrust, scorn and despair. Yet they can be hopeful of the return of their multicultural existence:

> Not many people slept in Mano Majra that night. They went from house to house—talking, crying, swearing love and friendship, assuring each other that this would soon be over. Life, they said, would be as it always had been. (153-54)

Finally, the Muslim community starts packing their belongings with tears in their eyes. The feeling of cultural rootlessness and dislocation upset them. Slowly, all the Muslims begin to come out of their homes. But the Sikh brothers with their dripping wet eyes promise the Muslim officer: "We will not touch our brothers' properties...we are brothers and will always remain brothers" (156). This speaks a lot about multiculturalism, but the tragedy of partition made them separate. Finally, the Muslims drive their bullock carts loaded with charpoy, rolls of bedding, tin trunks, kerosene oil tins, earthen pitchers and brass utensils. The Muslim officer tells them to be ready to go to Chundunnugger, a safe place for Muslim refugees. He announces: "All Muslims going to Pakistan come out at once. Come! All Muslims. Out at once" (155). He drives his jeep round the convoy and directs his Muslim brothers to say good-bye to their Sikh colleagues. "Mano Majra Sikhs and Muslims looked on helplessly" (159). With a heavy heart, all Muslims and Sikhs say good-bye to each other. The following extract shows their emotional involvement:

> The convoy slushed its way towards Chundunnugger. The Sikh watched them till they were out of sight. They wiped the tears off their faces and turned back to their homes with heavy hearts. (159)

The partition is not simply the tragedy of a nation but the tragedy of a group of innocent people who have fostered the values of multiculturalism. The above pathetic scene reminds us that partition has spoiled the peaceful life of communities which were quite ignorant of the adverse impact of British rule. In this regard, K.V. Surendran (2000: 74) says: "The Sikhs, Muslims and Hindus lived in a perfect harmony in this village and there was a time when no one in the village knew that the British had left the country and the country was divided into Pakistan and Hindustan."

In pre-partition Punjab, Sikhs and Muslims have consciously formed and maintained a stable multicultural society based on the principles of multiculturalism, i.e. peaceful coexistence, cultural plurality, religious diversity, recognition of differences, communal harmony, mutual trust, cultural tolerance and right to enjoy distinctive ways of life. In a sense, in pre-partition Punjab, all communities, irrespective of their culture and religion, were enjoying the fruits of multiculturalism. They had adopted and recognized the socio-cultural differences and maintained the law of social equality. But partition dislocates and uprootes them from their soil where they were born and brought up. What is significant is that even when they part physically from Mano Majra, the Sikhs and Muslims are able to reaffirm their faith in the finer values of human relationship.

The tragedy of partition does not end with the evacuation of the Muslims from Mano Majra. "Mano Majra's cup of sorrow was not yet full" (159). The entire village turns up for the evening prayers at the Gurudwara. After the prayer, a young Sikh boy enters in a hall with his friends. He looks quite aggressive and bossy. In the meeting, he expresses his anger against the Muslims:

> Our problem is: what are we to do with all these pigs we have with us? They have been eating our salt for generations and see what they have done! We have treated them like our brothers. They have behaved like snakes. (144)

The images like brother and snake suggest a possible opposition and rivalry between the two communities. As a representative of the Sikh community, he tries in his own strange way to illuminate the idea of communal harmony that will help them to escape from the coming danger of communal riot in the village. He argues furiously: "Are you all dead?" (169), "Is this a Sikh village?" (170), "What sort of Sikhs are you?" (170). These questions show the boy's hostility with the Muslim community. Therefore, he continues to attack the coolness and passivity of the Sikhs. His violent idea of communal harmony incites young Sikh boys who are cognizant about their religious, communal and cultural identities. As a result, a deep-rooted idea of brotherhood easily gets disrupted and finally the boy pulls out the weapon of communal identity. By referring to the stories of massacres and riots, he appeals to the volatile young Sikh boys:

> Do you know how many trainloads of dead Sikhs and Hindus have come over? Do you know of the massacres in Rawalpindi and Multan, Gujranwala and Sheikhupura? What are you doing about it? You just eat and sleep and you call yourselves Sikhs—the brave Sikhs! The martial class! He added, raising both his arms to emphasize his sarcasm. (170)

Now the politics of projecting false communal identity raises its ugly head. So far the elders from the Sikh community have shown sympathy, humanity and compassion to their old Muslim friends, but now the young Sikh boys become more conscious of their communal identity. The Sikh boy, the leader of the group, blames the other Sikhs for being passive and unreceptive. He poses a question before the Sikh boys: Are you "Potent or impotent?" (170). He tries to incite them further by telling stories of massacres and riots in the other parts of the country. He utters every word carefully to rouse their communal passion. He overlooks the accommodative and less aggressive nature of the Sikh religion. His inciting words make them more conscious of their communal identity. He intentionally pricks their pride by mocking at their inactive way of life.

By presenting this rabid character perhaps Khushwant Singh wants to advocate the significance and strength of the communal identity, a collective social strength. Multiculturalism recognizes values of communal identity which is to be protected and respected for maintaining social peace and integrity. The Muslims in Pakistan bluntly violate this principle. After partition, the Muslims in Pakistan behave like animals. Their animal like behavior causes great problems to the Muslims of Mano Majra. Thus, as an ideology, multiculturalism always promotes the value of identity that may be communal, religious or cultural. But after partition, the ideology of multiculturalism gets perverted and it becomes ugly, because of the misbehavior and disrespect of some people to other communities.

Though the rash boy decides to take revenge on the Muslim community, Meet Singh, a man of humanitarian concerns, tries to pacify the boy by making an emotional appeal: "What have the Muslims here done to us for us to kill them in revenge for what Muslims in Pakistan are doing? Only people who have committed crimes should be punished" (171). Further, he explains how the Muslims, born and brought up in this village, have shared and exchanged each other's sorrow and happiness. So according to him, there is no point in killing them in revenge. But the reckless young Sikh boy is not ready to listen. He subdues him with a series of angry outbursts: "What had the Sikhs and Hindus in Pakistan done that they were butchered? Weren't they innocent?" (171-72). His counter arguments show his antipathy to Muslims. Therefore, he gives a call for volunteers to make his plot successful:

> He spoke slowly, emphasizing each sentence by stabbing the air with his forefinger, 'for each Hindu or Sikh they kill, kill two Mussulmans. For each woman they abduct or rape, abduct two. For each home they loot, loot two. For each trainload of dead they send over, send two across. For each road convoy that is attacked, attack two. That will stop the killing on the other side. It will teach them that we can also play this game of killing and looting'. (171)

Each word of his speech is calculated to incite communal hatred and antipathy. His anti-human way of appealing to his fellow beings is a result of partition. He burns in the flames of Muslim antagonism. He expresses his anger: "I do not care. It is enough for me to know that they are Muslims. They will not cross this river alive" (173). The words like kill, abduct, rape, loot and attack clearly shows how friendship is replaced by enmity, reverence by disrespect, integrity by dishonesty, recognition by unfamiliarity. The overall change in the village and youngsters' aggressiveness shock the elders of Sikh community. But they are helpless and cannot hold against the flood of communal disharmony and social disintegration. Meet Singh weakly says: "I am an old bhai; I could not lift my hands against anyone—fight in battle or kill the killer. What bravery is there in killing unarmed innocent people?" (172). The elder Sikhs remain cool and silent before the young boys who are more conscious of their communal identities. Now due to partition, a cold war begins between two communities on the line of majority and minority. In Mano Majra, the Sikhs are in majority, whereas Muslims are few in number. In the final part of the novel, tolerance and respect to communal differences and identities are replaced by hatred, intolerance, prejudice and antipathy only because of a single divisive word called partition.

The storm of partition shatters not only the socio-cultural, socio-religious synchronization and integrity of Mano Majra, but also the inter-caste and inter-community relations. Jugga, a Sikh budmash, falls in love with Nooran, a Muslim weaver's daughter. But their love also melts in the fire of partition. The following extract reveals Jugga's love for the girl:

> 'Nooro, will you come tomorrow?' he asked, pleading. 'You think of tomorrow and I am bothered about my life. You have your good time even if I am murdered.' 'No one can harm you while I live. No one in Mano Majra can raise his eyebrows at you and get away from Jugga. I am not a budmash for nothing,' said he haughtily. (25-26)

Jugga and Nooron try to break the boundaries of community, religion and culture and foster their love. He expects her to be at the same place next day. But she is quite anxious about the conservative and conventional society and culture in which she is born. Jugga promises her not to be worried about any social pressure such as caste, community, religion or culture. His promising words show how open and bold enough he is to continue his relation with Nooran. He is less conscious of religion, caste and culture. In fact, Jugga-Nooran love affair bridges the gap between two communities in terms of difference in culture, religion, ideology and social standing. Their inter-community love affair is a sign of social change. In a sense, Jugga and Nooran have cherished the values of multiculturalism. After all, love knows no communal and religious boundary. Though Jugga and Nooran are representatives of two different communities, cultures and religions, their love grows beyond all differences.

Unfortunately, their love affair also ends with partition. Partition separates them forever. Thus, Jugga's final act shows his sacrifice for love and humanism, two of the basic values of Sikhism. As a religion, Sikhism is like needle and thread, which stitches the patches of caste, community and culture. Therefore, Khushwant Singh ends his narrative with the noteworthy act of Jugga's saving the lives of thousands of Muslims. His sacrifice is not only a result of his love for his beloved, but also his compassion, sympathy and kindness to the Muslim brothers who are on their way to Pakistan to resettle themselves. Multiculturalism, an accommodative social policy, encourages the principle of unity in diversity in multicultural societies and discourages hatred and violence based on ethnicity and religion. Perhaps Khushwant Singh wants to point up the value of multiculturalism, so he ends up his narrative with an elaborate description of Jugga's sacrifice for non-violence, love, humanism and respect to all.

He also presents the disfigured socio-religious face of India. He makes Hukumchand, a district magistrate, who describes India's fractured and broken socio-religious diversity:

> Take religion. For the Hindu, it means little besides caste and cow protection. For the Muslim, circumcision and kosher meat. For the Sikh, long hair and the hatred of the Muslim. For the Christian, Hinduism with a sola topee. For the Parsi, fire-worship and feeding vultures. Ethics, which should be the kernel of a religious code, has been carefully removed. Take philosophy, about which there is so much hoo-ha. It is just muddle-headedness masquerading as mysticism. (195-96)

The above extract reveals how India's socio-religious diversity is stippled by partition. Before partition, India was a home of different religions like Hindu, Muslim, Sikh, Christian, Parsi and all. All had maintained and retained their religious and cultural differences in terms of ethics, principles, ideologies and various ways of life. Without any friction and communal hatred, they respected and welcomed all those differences. But partition made them separate on the basis of religion. In a sense, partition developed a feeling of religious and communal hatred among different groups. People began to behave intolerantly towards each other's religious practices and their different ways of life. Obviously, religious respectability is replaced by communal hatred. Therefore, partition unnecessarily disturbed the religious faith of different people and gave birth to religious intolerance and communal hatred.

To sum up, the second line of analysis shows how the ideology of multiculturalism gets disrupted and destroyed after partition. The storm of partition has made people culturally and socially separate. The clouds of suspicion and intolerance hover over the village Mano Majra. Partition not only spoils the peaceful life of the masses but also dislocates them from the soil where they were born and bred. It has brought misery, distrust, antipathy, enmity, disrespect, despair and disharmony. Therefore, multiculturalism grew weaker and diluted in post-partition period.

4

Multiculturalism in *Bye Bye Blackbird*

Anita Desai is a leading Indian woman novelist in English. She is seriously concerned with the emotions, thoughts and cultural identities of her characters. Her novel *Bye Bye Blackbird* deals with Indian immigrants' problems in the alien land of England. Before 1960, England had adopted multiculturalism as a policy to attract 'outsiders' or 'others' because England was in need of unskilled and uneducated workers for her material growth and economic prosperity. However, England has also accepted multiculturalism as a political weapon for ruling people of different cultures and backgrounds. In the post-war period, people from all around the world with different cultures, backgrounds, religions, mentalities, histories and aspirations have flocked to England, a land of economic prosperity and opportunity. Thousands of Indians and other migrants from various countries arrived in England in search of blue-collar jobs in the growing industries. As K.N. Malik (1997: 91) rightly says: "The immigrants were inspired to migrate by Britan's post-war shortage of labour, its expanding economy and the portrayal of Britain as a land of 'great opportunity' by those who had come to the UK through army and navy connections."

The ethnic groups of various countries began to subdivide themselves according to their linguistic, cultural and religious identities. As a result, England turned out to be a large multicultural society. Interestingly, the diverse cultural groups retained/preserved their cultural and religious identities. They were very much conscious of their cultural, religious and ethnic identities in England. They asserted their identities by building gurudwaras, mosques and temples. These spiritual centers manifested their religious freedom and autonomy.

The migration of various non-white groups to England after 1960 had a number of important consequences. England started facing some serious problems due to the large inflow of the migrants. The natives believed that the immigrants as outsiders would invade their culture. So England, being a host country, changed its earlier policy of multiculturalism. As a result, the large numbers of colored (Asian) immigrants were paid less and were often discriminated against on the basis of color, caste, origin and religion. Such racial discrimination led to constant friction. Further, England started its policy of not accommodating and respecting 'other' alien cultures in its mainstream British culture.

In Anita Desai's novel, *Bye Bye Blackbird*, we see a continuous shift between the Oriental and Occidental culture. In the eyes of the Orientals, Occidental culture is more rational and superior which is characterized by logical thinking, tolerance, progress, modernism, independence and peace. However, Occidentals believe that Orientals are primitive, black, savage, violent, fanatic, underdeveloped, traditional and conservative. This has created a permanent rival relation of superiority-inferiority complex between the Occidentals and Orientals. With the help of their mass media, Occidentals have disarmed and neutralized the Orientals and labeled them as 'others' or 'outsiders'. In power relations, Occidentals have placed Orientals at the periphery and maintained their centrality at a global level. Thus, Orientals become the victims of western ideologies and philosophies, which conceive Europe as a symbol of supremacy of power and civilization. In the post-colonial period, too, the clash between the Oriental and Occidental culture continues. In fact, there is a continuous domination of the Occidental culture over the Oriental in the name of acculturation. This is a blatant violation of the international assumption that each culture is autonomous and free to retain its colors and flavors. The dominance of one culture over the other leads to social disharmony, unrest and friction. Edward Said in his seminal book, *Orientalism* expresses his view on the distinction between the Oriental sense of inferiority and Occidental superiority. Edward said (1991: 42) believes that: "Orientalism is better grasped as a set of constraints upon and limitations of thought than it is simply as a positive doctrine. If the essence of Orientalism is the ineradicable distinction between Western superiority and Oriental inferiority, then we must be prepared to note how in its development and subsequent history Orientalism deepened and even hardened the distinction."

Anita Desai has successfully depicted Asian immigrants' problems, especially those of Indian immigrants in England. The immigrants from Asian countries were known as 'blackbirds' in the land of white people. In the novel, she presents blackbirds as marginalized, dislocated, rejected and unwanted foreigners staying in a country that has not adopted and accepted them honestly. The feelings of alienation, emptiness and barrenness disturb their lives. The novel opens with the arrival of Dev, Adit's friend, in England. Adit is an Indian immigrant, married to Sarah, a British girl. Their inter-racial marriage invites clash between two cultures-Oriental and Occidental. She is sandwiched and squeezed between two different cultural forces. By creating the character of Dev, Anita Desai has shown Indians' disregard for and disrespect to British culture. Initially, he is disturbed and distressed by the prejudiced manners and the racial discrimination of the British people towards Indian immigrants. But gradual changes may be noticed in the attitudes of both Dev and Adit during the course of the novel. By marrying a black Asian, Sarah has broken the social conventions and codes of British culture, which is supposedly superior to and more refined than other cultures.

Throughout Desai's novel, we see the continuous ebb and flow of ideas in the minds of different characters. But the present study analyses the novel from sociological perspectives in order to see how multiculturalism is either reflected or deflected in the novel. The in-depth analysis of the novel reveals diverse themes: Adit's fascination and disregard for Occidental culture, Dev's contempt for Occidental culture, racial discrimination, prejudice, cultural intolerance, narrow-mindedness, problems of inter-racial/inter-cultural marriage, identity crisis, social ostracization/marginalisation, cultural rootlessness, socio-cultural conflicts, acceptance/rejection/adjustment and oscillation between Oriental/Eastern and Occidental/Western culture. Often we do not find a continuous flow of narration in the novel because of such psychological changes within the characters.

Adit, the protagonist of *Bye Bye Blackbird*, leads a settled life as an immigrant in London with his English wife Sarah, a leading female character of the novel. Adit is first of all fascinated by the Occidental culture and then disillusioned by it. Initially he regards England as a "land of opportunity" (19) and material prosperity. Thus, we see Adit being very critical of everything Indian. He says: "Nothing ever goes right at home—there is famine or flood, there is drought or epidemic, always" (129). His fascination for Occidental culture reveals his colonial hangover of valuing and respecting British culture as one that is more rational and advanced than the Oriental culture. J.P. Tripathi (1986: 44) has rightly explained Adit's love for Occidental culture: "Love of England and the Occident is exemplified through love of English society and its order and employment opportunity and economic and social and political freedom, love of English literature, English History, English Architecture and monuments, museums, Towers of victory and churches, English and Western Art and Painting and Picture Galleries of the past and the present, love of English countryside and nature, topography and rivers and valleys and the vegetations".

However, his fascination for the Occidental culture remains fresh only till the middle of the novel. His debate with his friend, Dev, exhibits his initial fascination for British culture. As an Asian immigrant, he sharply criticizes Indian ways of life but appreciates British culture:

> I love it here. I'm so happy here; I hardly notice the few drawbacks. I'll tell you—I did go back, three years ago, when I got engaged to Sarah and my parents wanted me to come with her. I stayed there looking for a job for four months. All I could find was a ruddy clerking job in some Government of India tourist bureau...I'm happy here...I like the Convent Garden opera house...I feel like millionaire. I like the girls here...I used to like dancing with them...I like thatched cottages and British history and reading the letters in The Times. I like the pubs. I like the freedom a man has here: Economic freedom! Social freedom! I like reading the posters in the tube...I like weekend at the seaside. I even like the BBC! He ended with a shout of triumph. (17-18)

According to him, while the Occident promotes autonomy and liberty, the Orient is an embodiment of restrictions and limits. What one notices in him is a kind of fascination for a seemingly superior culture which is indicative of his colonial hangover. If his own country symbolizes a passive and sluggish life, the British society is vibrant in all its aspects: "...here there is no death at all. Everything—animal, vegetable, mineral—is alive, rich and green forever" (129). To Adit, things are really bright in England, "Here the rain falls so softly and evenly, never too much and never too short. The sun is mild. The earth is fertile. The rivers are full. The birds are plump. The beasts are fat. Everything so wealthy, so luxuriant—so fortunate" (129). It shows Adit's obsession for Occidental culture that separates him from his 'home' culture. Adit has moulded and transformed himself entirely up to the expectations of England.

The other reasons for Adit's admiration for England are social, political and beauraucratic. Thus, he points out that there is no corruption or bribe in England. He feels "the magic of England—her grace, her peace, her abundance and the embroidery of her history and traditions" (157). Further, the clerks of England, unlike their Indian counterparts, are not lazy and he does not have to be bothered by unpunctuality of trains and buses.

What England offers to him is a carefree life that suits a sybarite. What India offers him is a life of inconveniences and a difficult style of existence. But he enjoys the life of a bourgeois in England, which offers him pubs, women to eye and a lot of wine. England for him is a symbol of refinement and sophistication, while India is a home of crudities and dirt. The more he compares his own culture with that of England, the more Anglophile he becomes.

Adit's fascination for British culture is not so objectionable, but the way he looks at his 'home' culture is not acceptable in the light of the theory of multiculturalism, because multiculturalism acknowledges cultural equality, recognition of differences and disapproves the dominance of one culture over the other.

As a person who loves and admires England, "her history and her poetry as much as any Englishman" (164), Adit is too critical of his own fellow countrymen in England. His rude comments on Dev's behavior and his Indian thinking illustrate this fact: "If anyone suggested going to the coffee house, it was you who pointed out that no one had money. If anyone thought of going for a moonlight drive, you pointed out that there was no moon and none of us had a car. You think black by habit" (19). What is obnoxious in Adit's behavior is his inability to acknowledge the fact that he himself is a product of Indian culture and that any imitation of English ways cannot make him a native of that country. It may also be argued that his Anglophilia is a consequence of his admiration for his own wife Sarah: "I see gold—everywhere—gold like Sarah's golden hair" (19).

While admiring the history and poetry of the west, Adit seems to forget, rather willingly, the fact that the British have used them to play up their hegemony and maintain their central position at a global level. They have been able to project the idea that what is Occidental is good and desirable and when the idea catches up with the subservient attitude of people like Adit, the task of the white men—to colonize the mind of the Third World—becomes easier. If Adit has greater admiration for the history and poetry of England than those of his own, then it implies the hegemonic success of the West over its blind cultural fans.

What is striking about Adit's initial Anglophilia is his utter disregard for what is native, what is his own. Over the years, the white men have done everything possible to belittle all that is non-European. What one notices in this kind of intellectual superciliousness is their reluctance to acknowledge the value of multiculturalism, the significance of minorities' identities. Indians like Adit, at least for a while, fall a prey to the glitter of the white ideology of art, philosophy and life. The fact that he gets out of his obsession with everything white itself is a testimony to the hollowness of the white ideology. It also points up the fact that cultures can educate you when you attempt to study them more from close quarters and experience them by living in them. This is illustrated in the attitudinal transformation that takes place in Adit's mind.

Dev, Adit's friend, comes to England for studying at the London School of Economics. Initially he is averse and reluctant to the idea of staying on in England as an immigrant. But gradually a slow change occurs in the attitude of Dev. His initial encounter with British people and their culture brings unhappiness and discontent. The cultural differences expand when Dev moves about in search of a job. He undergoes various experiences and cultural shocks. The difference between expectation and reality upsets him and makes him self-conscious and insecure. As he says, "I wouldn't live in a country where I was insulted and unwanted" (17). He wishes to go back to India as an "England-returned teacher" (17). He comes all the way to London for a proper education. But in London, he feels to be an unnamed stranger facing various socio-cultural problems. In his desperate mood, he calls Adit, his friend "a spineless imperialist-lover" (19). He openly calls London "a jungly city" (10), where people live in their own cocoons without any social concern. Every encounter in London prompts Dev to compare the differences between Eastern and Western cultures (Oriental-Occidental). He observes the neighbors' silence, "their radios, their quarrels, their children are all kept behind closed doors" (56). This kind of cultural difference shocks him. Therefore, he feels isolated in an alien land:

> If this were India...I would by now know all my neighbors—even if I had never spoken to them. I'd know their taste in music by the sound of their radios. I'd know the age of their child by the sound of its howling. I'd know if the older children were studying for exams by the sound of lessons being recited. (56)

It is true that there are hundreds of Third World immigrants in London who willfully forget the value of their own local cultures in the glitter of the western city. But Dev has been able to perceive the loneliness that lurks beneath the sheen of the city. Every individual in the urban center is alienated from his neighbor. What one notices is a breakdown of any soul-to-soul communication. If an Englishman cannot have real communication with another Englishman, then how can he establish any meaningful relationship with an immigrant who is a black or brownie? The white man's lack of concern for others is symbolized in the 'closed door' referred to in Desai's novel. Dev's confrontation with western indifference, unlike in the case of Adit, is the sudden realization that his own culture is accommodative; it is concerned about others' problems and personal sorrows. Individuals' sorrows in India can be the neighbours' too. And what Dev desires is a transplantation of his own cultural values to England (West). He wishes for the establishment of Indian religious centers and the transference of Indian religious gurus to England.

Indeed there is no dearth of moral and religious ideas, such as 'love thy neoghbour as thyself'; in England but in the race for attaining material success, the white man has forgotten the value of such ideas. But what Dev notices is the practice of similar ideas in his own country. Material prosperity and superiority complex have taken away the emotions of love and concern for the other, thereby downplaying the relevance of multiculturalism. What Dev witnesses in England is social disharmony and stratification of cultures. The eagerness to be secluded and unconcerned is visible everywhere and, consequently, what one notices even in a busy city like London is emptiness. And Dev notices this:

> Another thing to which Dev cannot grow accustomed, in all his walks and bus rides through the city is silence and emptiness of it—the houses and blocks of flats, streets and squares and crescents—all, to his eyes and ears, dead, unalive, revealing so little of the lives that go on, surely must go on, inside them. The English habit of keeping all doors and windows tightly shut...of guarding their privacy.... It never fails to make Dev uneasy to walk down a street he knows to be heavily populated and yet find it utterly silent, deserted—a cold wasteland of brick and tile. (63)

Dev's Anglophobia, thus, is a result of his intense observation of English life. The seclusion of the white man is often considered as his introspective nature. But if such introspection does not lead to the self-discovery that every human being has individuality, then it is a meaningless self-analysis. What one needs to discover is the connection of one's self with the other. Then multiculturalism, in spite of the diverse elements in it, can be a reality. Appreciation of a different individual is the appreciation of a different culture. And what is lacking in a multicultural society like England is this accommodation of a different culture or the openness of a liberal mind. Consequently, as Dev notices, the city can offer only a sense of emptiness to the inhabitants. What he is aware is the close ties that exist in his own country, which is much more multilingual and multicultural than any European country, between people even in a sparsely populated locality. And that is a noteworthy difference between the Occident and the Orient.

This difference is acknowledged even by the British as a response of Sarah, Adit's wife, reveals. When Dev questions the unashamed behaviour of the lovers in Hyde Park, while they make a show of their love ignoring the passers-by, Sarah replies: "English people aren't as self-conscious as they are supposed to be" (65). They are not self-conscious because they are cocooned in their own places of dwelling. The Dev-Sarah discussion on the lovers' behaviour reveals further the vast cultural differences that exist between the East and the West.

Here the comparison between Oriental and Occidental cultures is not so important, but cultural differences should be recognized positively if they do not cause harm to social peace and harmony. After all, each culture has something new and valuable to share with others, but sharing cultural differences should not necessarily lead to social crumbling and disintegration. As a social theory, multiculturalism centers around the basic idea that every culture presents only a limited range of worldviews. The assistance of other cultures is required not only to understand the world better, but also to enrich its own culture and expand the horizon of general understanding. Therefore, no culture is wholly worthless; each carries some value for its members. This also suggests that no culture is perfect. So multiculturalism prioritizes cultural pluralism and sensitizes the dangers of cultural majoritarianism or dominance.

However, Dev also does not seem to acknowledge fully the value of multiculturalism. He assigns himself the role of a cultural ambassador to India:

> I am here, he intoned, as an ambassador. I am showing these damn imperialists with their lost colonies complex that we are free people now, with our own personalities that this veneer of an English education has not obscured, and not afraid to match ours with theirs'. I am here... to interpret my country to them, to conquer England as they once conquered India, to show them, to show them. (123)

But he is performing his role as ambassador with vengeance in mind. The expression 'these damn imperialists' bears this out. He is proud of the harmony and peace that exist in his country even though it is highly multicultural in its composition. There is an element of arrogance in his outburst and it causes him to downplay the sharp divisions that have existed in his country along the lines of caste and religion. What he desires now is a cultural invasion of England. His scorn for the Englishman's 'white' superiority consciousness is understandable. His assertion that English language and literature were white man's weapon for colonizing the Indian mind is also justifiable. But his desire to colonize the cultural thinking of the west is essentially wrong, for multiculturalism does not rest on the principle of an eye for an eye and tooth for a tooth. What is acceptable is Dev's critique of the continuing impact of British hegemonic attitude. But his imaginary moral and cultural attack on the British is suggestive of his own colonial aspirations. In this sense his Anglophobia is unjustifiable. What is perhaps admirable in his anti-British stance is his decision to not to be a "Macaulay's Bastard" (122).

In another early outburst, Dev hopes to reverse the whole history of the British colonization of India. He imagines the Sikhs and the Sindhis going to England as traders and gradually consolidating their power there. He imagines the large-scale migration of Indians and the spreading of Indian ways, customs and manners there. He visualizes the establishment of temples and gurudwaras as also the exchange of Indian yogis and gurus in place of priests and patrons. He also imagines the replacement of Greek and Latin with Sanskrit and Punjabi swear words. In short, he wants 'history [to] turn the tables now' on England.

However, once again we notice the impracticality of Dev's colonial imaginings. It is very difficult for anyone to take history backwards again. History has its own course and even if it repeats, it repeats itself. Dev's notion of the Indian colonization of the West is slightly quixotic. While being in an alien land he had all the opportunities to be a native imitator of the west. But he has maintained his essential identity as an Indian. Yet, what is objectionable in his Indianness is his belief that everything Indian is good and everything British is bad. His hope to be a cultural ambassador in England does not seem to be impressive. The British has had the opportunity to confront a great cultural ambassador like Gandhi. Over the years many such ambassadors from various countries have tried to educate nations, including Britain, in the positive dimensions of multiculturalism. Further, even in India there has been frequent instances of violations of multicultural values. The subjugation of the dalits by the so-called upper class is a case in point.

However, if Dev is Desai's mouthpiece, then Dev's outbursts may be viewed as her legitimate postcolonial stance as a writer. Then Dev's utterances should be taken as examples of exaggeration meant to express her anti-colonial stance. They serve the purpose of bringing out the pain of subjugation and hegemony experienced by the colonized. She seems to point up the fact that all forms of colonization are a violation of the essential democratic principles of multiculturalism.

India was a British colony for nearly three centuries. During this long period, England could consolidate its political power and exploit the resources available here. Although Indians outnumbered the British rulers, political and military power enabled Britain to keep Indians as their subjects and wield her power freely. However, the position of the Indian immigrants has been different. They have always been controlled by the laws of the country. As the number of immigrants began to increase, the laws became stricter. It was the Englishman's necessity to keep the immigrants as a minority and thus overcome the fear of the latter outnumbering the local people. The white man's rigid immigration laws only curtailed the freedom of the Indian. As Viney Kirpal (1989: 247) says: "Englishmen's feeling of insecurity made them accuse the immigrants of having lowered their standard of living, of having deprived them of employment, of having fouled up their beautiful countryside, of having brought crime and disease to their land...and so on and so forth." The laws of the British government have often been discriminatory. They often manifest in society in various forms of discrimination based on race, color, origin and culture. A recent example of such racial bias is Shilpa Shetty's experience in England at the Big Brother reality show.

The suppressed racial antagonism against the Asian immigrants is a result of the white man's long-established belief that he is superior to the non-white people. Edward Said's attitude to the Orient, as he argues, is shaped by his own people's history of the East. As such, Indians, along with other Asians, face inequality on the basis of colour and race. In such a society multiculturalism does not seem to have a healthy future. There the immigrants feel frustrated, alienated and marginalized.

These feelings find clear expression in Dev's antagonism towards everything British. To quote K. Jha (2004: 161-62): "*Bye Bye Blackbird* is full of situations in which we find characters struggling to survive the racial onslaught. Racial prejudice often gets expression through the accusation against the coloured immigrants for spreading dirt and filth." However, Adit's mother-in-law, a racist to the core, cannot accept her own Indian son-in-law and his Indian friends. When they enter her kitchen: "It was evident she was thinking that all she had heard about the filthy ways of the Asian immigrants was correct" (133). She "charged in, her face as flushed and her eyes as big as though she expected to find murder being committed in her kitchen" (157). What is evident in such remarks and instances in the novel is the age-old belief of the Occidentals that the culture of the Orient is primitive, filthy, inferior and dirty. The history of the Orient, as narrated by the historians of the West, is meant to consolidate European centrality and to depict the Third World as the 'Other'.

The peculiar kind of racism that prevails in England has a historical background. The colonial dominion of the British in India has given them a sense of superiority which comes in handy in the present when the erstwhile subjects are immigrants in their country. Desai's novel comments on this secure position of the Englishman. As P.K. Pandeya (2001: 20) puts it: "The novel touches on racial problems and feeling in England. This feeling becomes sharper when it comes to a colonizer nation like England who has ruled over us for a long time. It is not simply white man's burden but also the feeling of superiority by virtue of their being ruler over us."

Thus, Desai seems to imply that England cannot be a melting pot of cultures. It is a fertile ground for discrimination and marginalization of the Eastern people. The inherent craze of the ruling class once again manifests itself in the petty discriminatory feelings of Mrs. Simpson and Roscommon-James, Adit's mother-in-law.

Discrimination based on colour and race is treated with illustrations in *Bye Bye Blackbird*. The shocking fact is that even the white children grow up with a warped knowledge of colour and race differences. Thus, while on a sightseeing trip to London, Dev is called a 'wog' by a schoolboy. Dev's reaction to the insult is sharp, but the point is the boy's awareness that anyone other than a white-skinned person can be insulted publicly. A little later we find Dev pointing out to Adit that "the London docks have three kinds of lavatories-Ladies, Gents and Asiatics" (17). Even nationality of an individual, thus, becomes a criterion for discrimination. In some cases, differences in race and colour can endanger the Asian immigrants' life. For instance, Mala, an immigrant woman, explains how her son reacts when he is chased by a gang of English children. He shouts at them in despair: "I'm not black! I'm not black-I'm grey!" (26). As Usha Bande (1991: 191) argues: "In *Bye Bye Blackbird* Anita Desai tackles issues pertaining to racial and cultural prejudices, adjustment and acceptance, and the subjective and objective views of a historical situation hard to shake off."

What the immigrant feels in England is the pressure of the dominant white culture on him. The natives of England have succeeded in marginalizing the immigrants and in intimidating them with their status of a minority. There is no culture in England for the immigrants to identify with. Their desperate attempts to get back to their roots and Indian identity (as in the case of Dev, for example) suggest their cultural rootlessness in Europe.

There are occasions when the immigrants' economic worth is judged by their origin and appearance. The fact is that the immigrant's white counterpart may be less rich and lower in employment status. Yet the latter's air of superiority is evident, it is often repulsive. The behaviour of the pedlar of Russian icons to Dev is a case in point. Dev's attempt to know the price of an icon is contemptuously ignored by the pedlar. Note this exchange between them on the price:

> 'How much?'
>
> 'Oh', says the young man, smiling with an infuriating kindness, 'it is expensive.'
>
> 'Yes. How much?' repeats Dev, more heatedly, on fire to possess an object which he has so far viewed with a detached and objective ardour.
>
> 'Very much', the man bites on the words as though they were thin threads, snap-snap, still smiling like a jocular alligator. 'Oh, very much. I wouldn't even name the price to you.' (71)

Dev is almost treated like an untouchable who is culturally backward and socially mean. However, what is bright about Dev's character is his ability to critique the hollowness of the white culture. The fact that he has married Sarah, a white woman, indicates that his anger is not aimed at the white human beings but at their superiority complex. What he expects of them is a certain degree of mutual concern and respect for the 'Other'. His irate outbursts are, in a sense, his challenges to the European cultural hegemony and an assertion of his faith in the inherent values of Indian culture, and, by extension, the relevance of other small cultures. What he seems to imply is that while asserting one's own culture, one can also maintain friendly relations with other cultures and minority groups. Multiculturalism promotes healthy dialogues between cultures, but what Dev is confronted with is prejudice, inequality, distrust, injustice and oppression.

The British in Desai's novels are so colour-conscious that even jobs are reserved for the fair-skinned Europeans. What is all the more shocking is how people are categorized according to their religion. Thus at an interview for a job, the interviewer informs Dev that the latter cannot be offered the job because he is not a Christian. And the interviewer openly speaks of the religious reservation of the job:

> Not a Catholic? Not even Christian? ...I am sorry. Dear me, I ought to have mentioned it at once...we simply must have a Catholic, or at least a High Church man.

> It's public relations...I'm afraid it wouldn't do to have a Hindu gentleman in this job. (108)

It now becomes evident that the white (European) hegemony is directed not only by cultural, social, racial and economic considerations but also by religious factors. The white woman Roscommon-James has no qualms about openly admitting religious priorities in giving jobs to people of other cultures and religions. Thus, she informs Dev that it is not easy for Indians to get a job in London, for "there are many people with right complexion, of course, but not for Indians" (149). What is overlooked by the European employers is the qualification of the candidate. They begin with the assumption that Indians are of a lesser intelligence and competence and that they cannot be offered all jobs. Once again, discrimination in professional opportunities is a characterizing feature of British/European hegemony. The very hegemonic nature of the West is a direct violation of all principles of multiculturalism. It fails to acknowledge the necessity of cultural diversity and promotes favouritism. The existence of different religious groups can be a feature of a multicultural society, but when people are discriminated against on the basis of their religions and national status; multicultural principles get violated very badly.

What is perhaps shocking is the attitude of the Europeans to racial discrimination and the casual way in which they take it as a normal event in their societies. When Adit's friend, for example, asks Mrs. Roscommon-James about a riot that takes place in a factory, she replies, rather unconcernedly: "Heavens, one of those racial things" (136). Desai reminds us of the treatment that Asian immigrants have been receiving from the imperialists. To the imperialists, the immigrants have been outsiders and the latter often protest which lead to riots and acts of xenophobia. The immigrants are a threat to the natives and rather than passing laws for peaceful coexistence, they indulge in acts which have no justification in a civil society.

However, it is significant that Desai doesn't permanently distrust the possibility of a proper multiculturalism even in the racially ravaged England. Sarah's marriage to Adit illustrates this point. By marrying Adit, a coloured Indian, Sarah has violated certain unwritten codes and conventions of the colour-conscious white society. At the surface level, the validity of such a marriage will not be challenged even by the rabid racists. They might remain silent for the sake of social propriety. But the silence is no indication of an approval of the marriage. Indeed nobody questions the validity of Adit-Sarah marriage. But once the marriage is over, she is humiliated not only by her colleagues at her school, where she is a secretary, but also by the pupils of the school. In this regard, N.R Gopal (1996: 175) says: "Sarah incurs the anger of the white society by marrying a brown Asian as she had broken the social code of England. Hence, she is always subject to taunts and comments of not only her colleagues but even of young pupils of the school." Her colleagues ask her about Adit and his family background. Julia, for instance, asks: "Your husband isn't going to stay here forever, is he?" (36). Her students pretend not to have seen her. When they see her, they warn one another, "Hurry, Hurry, Mrs. Curry" (34). Her colleagues want to know Adit's future plans, too. Thus, in her own country, which has had its dominion over many countries and cultures in the world including India, she cannot find any sign of mutual trust and cooperation. As Meenakshi Mukherjee (1978: 228) says: "Sarah is an unusual character who is displaced in her own country, whose crisis of identity will perhaps never be solved although she believes that going to India will be the final resolution of her ambiguous existence."

And this kind of humiliating existence has created in her a sense of alienation. The loneliness that she feels in her own white society becomes complete when even her parents extend a cold welcome to her and her husband on their first visit to her house after marriage. For the parents, it seems, the issue is that their daughter has married an Asian, the Other, with whom they cannot establish a heart-to-heart relationship. In fact, they maintain a feeling of aversion to him. Consider, for example, the father-in-law's reaction, which confuses Adit:

> Adit could not comprehend a parental relationship so cool that the parent did not rush out and embrace the daughter whom he had not seen since last Christmas,

> but kept himself out of her way as though he were avoiding her. He did not say this aloud—he had, in the past, sometimes mentioned his astonishment and disapproval of their colourless, toneless, flavourless relationship only to have Sarah say impatiently, 'Oh we can't stand cuddling and netting and all that!' to which Adit had protested, 'But your mother loves it when I give her a hug and a kiss,' and then was offended when Sarah gave a small snort of scorn. (142)

The father gives no sign of recognizing them or of being pleased by their visit. He has retired not only from his job but also from 'Sarah's life'. Such discriminatory treatment has made her feel marginalized. The taunts of colleagues, the contempt of students and the standoffishness of her own parents have had a weakening impact on her psyche. She doesn't dare to meet people like a normal human being. Like an outcaste, she avoids meeting people. Even for shopping she goes to distant places so that she can escape the accusing, jeering looks of her own people:

> She walked out into the soft, muzzling rain with her packages, reassured to find herself an unidentifiable, unnoticed and therefore free person again. The bus came and she found herself a seat next to the door so that she did not need to push past or touch anyone, and she turned her face to the blurred window, observing the melting greys and greens of the common with that fixed expression of stark loneliness that had so stirred her husband on another rainy afternoon. (39)

The irony is that she can't feel at home in the company of her own white fellow beings. Further she can feel her identity and freedom when she is amidst strangers. In a sense, she is homeless in her own native land, and that itself is a commentary on England's idea of multiculturalism.

However, what is striking about Sarah's character is that she does not like to be a passive sufferer for long. She faces marginalization at every place—home, school and society. In fact, these places are institutions, which are supposed to maintain human values and relations. Ironically, they have become places of hatred, spite, discrimination and contempt. They have cleaved Sarah's self and shattered all her sense of belonging. Any woman could become a nervous wreck in such a situation. Indeed she is shattered but she makes an earnest effort to piece together her shattered self. She realizes that unity of self can be achieved only by renouncing and denouncing her own culture and society, which are white and hegemonic. She wants to get back to her own identity as Sarah, although she is not unhappy with her identity as Mrs. Sen. The problem is Mrs. Sen is nobody, she is only a mask:

> Who was she—Mrs. Sen who had been married in a red and gold benares brocade sari one burning, bronzed day in September, or Mrs. Sen, the Head's secretary, who sent out the bills and took in the cheques, kept order in the school and was known for her efficiency? ...She was nobody. Her face was only a mask, her body only a costume. Where was Sarah? (34-35).

Surprisingly, unlike the typical white (wo)man, Sarah has great faith in the institution of marriage and the bond of love that has sustained it over centuries. For recreating her own identity and also for maintaining the validity of marriage, she decides to move out of her own country. She takes the path breaking decision of settling down in India, the land of her husband. It is a land; she seems to have understood, that still holds some respect for marital relationship. It is a land that has accommodated people of diverse backgrounds, cultures and religions for centuries. Further, it is a land that has been a shelter for the alien and the exile. Weakness though it may appear, the land was friendly even to the invaders (the Europeans) who were wolves in sheep's clothing.

Sarah's decision to adopt India as her homeland is an outcome of her feeling that "she had become nameless" (31). What she seeks is a land where she will not have to live with the silent fear of being indirectly ostracized. Since she has already "her ancestry and identity" (31), she needs a place where she can find humanity, kindness, fellow feeling and self-respect. As B.R. Parmar (2005: 36) says: "Sarah is homeless in her own homeland on account of her marriage with an

Oriental immigrant. Sarah is firm and fair in her commitments. She tries to be a sincere and loving wife to her husband. She does not want to destroy her conjugal life for the sake of her different cultural identity. She is so calm and composed that she never complains about anything either to her husband or to her parents. She does not like to remember her past. She wants to enjoy present with self-identity and self-respect."

It is significant that Sarah's decision matches Adit's disillusionment and disenchantment with English culture and manners. Bitter experiences in England teach him to respect his own country with all its weaknesses and drawbacks. If England has advanced civilizationally, it has failed to recognize human worth. What India's multiculturalism underscores, at least in principle, is the worth of a human being. In spite of all his 'love and regard' for England and self-hatred, England does not accept him (Adit). This realization of exclusion really hurts him.

Sarah's decision to move to India with her Indian husband has an element of protest in it. She is moving to a country that was ruled by her country in the recent past. As such her own people, with their hegemonic spirit, have been looking down upon the country and its people. But Sarah quite challengingly establishes a blood relation with an Indian and further adopts a British colony as her own motherland. When her own country disowns her, she makes her home in a country that England subjugated. In this she is joining the ally of the other and thus rises in revolt against the white assumptions of hegemony and superiority. Thus her marriage is a challenge while at the same time it is her means to blend the Occident with the Orient and thus suggest the possibility of multiculturalism that crosses the artificial boundaries of colour and creed laid by white hegemonic/dominant structures. These structures are represented by her own parents, her colleagues, students and the society at large.

There may be problems of adjustment awaiting Sarah in her new avatar as an Indian wife. But it is definitely more tolerable than the humiliations she experiences in her own country. Therefore, she has decided to face the problems with utmost coolness. She decides to play her role as a wife who can validate the merits of marriage. She leaves the theatre of artificialities (England) and enters the real world. Anita Desai has effectively developed Sarah's image as an Indian wife who accepts her husband with all his cultural, religious, social and ideological diversities. Though Sarah has her roots in British soil, her decision to embrace Indian culture is worth noting. By marrying an Asian immigrant, she has tried to convey a message to the plural world that the time has come to respect and value different cultures because the world is becoming a global village where everybody has his/her own significance and relevance. Therefore, Sarah's marriage symbolically underscores the need to accept and respect all kinds of diversities—cultural, religious, social and ideological and develops a sense of tolerance, patience, open-mindedness and forbearance.

Adit's disenchantment with English way of life is timely. Desai uses his frustration to emphasize the value of one's own cultural identity. Sarah loses her identity in her own homeland, while Adit loses it in an alien land. The mistake he commits is to create a false foreign identity in a hostile surrounding. The shocks he receives from various sources in England save him from damaging his self under the pressure of racial discrimination. His visit to his wife's house and the cold treatment he receives there is unbearable. He discovers that his mother-in-law hates and despises him. He feels "depression pouring into him like lead, hot when it entered in the form of Mrs. Roscommon-James' sniffs and barks..." (176). At one of the gatherings, Bella calls him an 'Indian', a 'foreigner' and a 'dirty Asian'. He realizes that he cannot be a normal human being in England. He even asks:

> Why does everything have to come to this—that we're Indians and you're English and we're living in your country and therefore we've all go to behave in a special way, differing from normal people? (187-88)

So Adit's problem is living an artificial life in the midst of standardized mores and manners. When he behaves in the most natural way he is branded as a dirty Asian. The values of his own culture do not get any respect among the white men. Confronting to the pretentious and unreal way of English life is a serious problem. The sense of alienation and marginalization becomes so acute in him that he realizes his mistake of being an anglophile all these years. The transformation now is from anglophilia to anglophobia. The latter feeling finds expression in his decision to leave England for good with his wife. He informs her and asks her if she will follow him:

> I can't live here any more. Our lives here—they've been so unreal, don't you feel it? Little India in London. All our records and lamb curries and sing-songs, it's all so unreal. It has not reality at all; we just pretend all the time. I'm twenty-seven now. I've got to go home and start living a real life. I don't know what real life there will mean. I can't tell you if it won't be war, Islam, communism, famine, anarchy or what. Whatever it is it will be Indian, it will be my natural condition, my true circumstance. I must go and face all that now. It's been wonderful here. Sarah, you know I've loved England more than you, I've often felt myself half-English, but it was only pretence, Sally. Now it has to be a real thing. I must go. You will come? (203-04)

It is heartening to witness this transformation of Adit. Desai carefully politicizes his experience by bringing it in the broad context of colonization. Thus, she wishes that Adit's shaking off of a hegemonic impact should be ideally the move that every Indian should take. The novelist thus moves from the particular to the general. England is presented as 'an aggressor' who has 'tried to enmesh, subjugate and victimize him with the weapons of Empire'. The significance of Adit's transformation lies in his successful attempt to break away from all bondages of the Empire. England, Adit's 'once-golden Mecca' has now taken the form of the proverbial colonizer who is opportunistic, brutal and cold. Adit's decision is the revolt of the colonized. What is commendable is Sarah's willingness to share his decision to wriggle out of the clutches of the colonizer. Both have suffered on account of their skin colour and inter-racial marriage. Sarah warmly sympathizes with him, because she has seen his whole personality cracking "apart into an unbearable number of disjointed pieces, rattling together noisily and disharmoniously" (200). She takes up the painstaking responsibility of piecing together his crumbling personality. Yes, she has her apprehensions about her new life in an alien land. Yet she is optimistic: "I think when I go to India; I will not find it so strange after all. I am sure I shall feel quite at home very soon" (219). She consolidates her hope practically by suggesting, "Let's have an Indian meal tonight" (179). Even before reaching India she can compare the life in England with that of India. In her own country, "everyone is a stranger and lives in hiding. They live silently and invisibly. It would happen nowhere in India" (56).

Adit still has doubt about her willingness to leave her country and hence he poses the question, "Could you really leave all this, Sally, and go away to India to live?" (83). And her answer is an emphatic 'yes'. So Adit finds a partner in his revolt and the purpose of their rebellion is the establishment of true multiculturalism, which has international dimensions. With her, Adit is going to carry a message:

> And how he was going to carry the message of England to the East—not the old message of the colonist, the tradesman or the missionary, but the new message of the free convert, the international citizen, a message of progress and good cheer, advance and good will. (225-26)

Their new message bears the multicultural principle of peaceful coexistence. Significantly, Adit who returns to India as a cultural ambassador has no grudge against the country of the white. And that indeed is a Gandhian attitude.

Anita Desai does not wish to suggest that multiculturalism is impossible in England. The activities of the character Emma, an English lady, illustrate this fact. She is an ardent fan of Indian culture. Very early in the novel, we read about her decision to start a club:

> A little Indian club to which my Indian friends could come on Wednesday afternoons—I choose Wednesday

> because it always rains and strangers would be happy to have somewhere to go and have something to do. They could meet some really interested, intelligent English people and tell them, teach them about India. (41-42)

She is able to address Indians as her friends. She has recognized the value of Indian spirituality and has decided to "give lessons in Yoga too" (42). The club has no materialistic concerns because, according to Emma, "there will be no money transactions at all in my club" (42). She wants the club members to learn from famous Indians: "Then, when famous Indians visit London—philosophers or painters or musicians—we shall invite them to come and address the Little India club" (42-43). Emma is at least making an attempt to recognize the value of another culture—the culture of a former colony of her own imperialist country.

Matriarchal value system is not something that is not well appreciated in India. Yet Anita Desai's Sikh lady upholds the merits of matriarchy. The lady is generous and munificent. Her prime intention is to enable the immigrants from India to feel at home in the strange land of England. She is well aware of the pains of the rootless immigrants. Her matriarchal dominance is positive and encouraging. On one occasion she admonishes Dev for not seeking her help:

> And you did not come to us for help? What is this—are we not neighbors? Am I not like your own mother? It is bad you have not thought of coming to me and calling me mother. I am here to be mother to all our poor Indian boys lost and alone in this cold country. And my sons—such strong young men—can't they help you? Each one of them has a good job, a good pay. Every week they bring their full salary to me. I divide it into three parts—one for their own pockets for they are my sons and I must keep them happy, one for the household, and the third, the largest, for our family and our land in Punjab. (118)

The warmth and love she exudes have wiped out the authoritarianism of the matriarch. While seclusion, privacy and fear of the other characterize western life, here is a lady who encourages people to maintain fellow feeling and mutual concern. She, too, upholds the merits of cultural accommodation.

Indeed we come across such instances through which Desai underscores the greatness of multiculturalism, which is essentially Indian. Yet she has no illusory belief that the fabric of Indian multiculturalism is strong. Rather, she seems to assert that multiculturalism is possible only when the parties involved have the readiness to forget and forgive. She also seems to believe that multiculturalism can be maintained only with difficulty. The picture of India outside is rosy and romantic, but it is not really so. Desai makes Adit say it for the knowledge of Sarah who is going with him to India with much hope:

> ...that romantic India in which all flowers were perfumed, all homes harmonious and every day a festival. 'She's not going to live in a maharaja's palace, you know. She's going to live in a family of in-laws, a very big one, and learn their language and habits. (213)

The family she is going to is a microcosm of the culturally diverse India. It is large, there are people with conventional and modern viewpoints and there are also chances of friction. Yet such large families still survive; they show how this difficult balance of diversity/differences is maintained. Like these families, India too has maintained the balance of cultures, religions, sects, beliefs and opinions although it has been occasionally made upset by intolerant groups. Shedding of ego, adjustment to unknown set-ups and respecting others' sentiments are the essential factors that have contributed to the continued existence of multiculturalism in India. Desai says as much. The Sikh lady, for instance, tells Sarah that if the latter has to be happy in India, she has to be "an Indian wife, an Indian daughter-in-law" (218). The old lady perceives typical Indian qualities in Sarah: "When I look at you, when I see you going out in the morning and coming home, always so quiet with your head bent, not looking at anyone, then I think you are one of our own.... You will see it is your own country" (218). Sarah has already shed her English ego to adjust herself to a society that has certain cultural norms. Certainly, this kind of submission suggests colonial tendencies, yet they are necessary for the maintenance of harmony and unity.

True, such Indian set-up, where submission is a pre-condition, has its drawbacks. Yet there is an air of informality and freedom in the Indian way of life. Many things which are too formal (including family relations) and time-bound in the West are pleasantly loose and carefree in India. Violations of time do not always invite the wrath of others. There is a kind of timelessness in India, which may be irritating to the west, but forgetting the clock often strengthens human ties. Infringing the dictate of the clock is a way of culturally distinguishing the Oriental from the Occidental. Entering a bar late in the night, with Dev, for a bottle of beer, Adit succinctly puts it across to the bar man:

> You must admit that it is the trouble with Orientals—we don't really believe in watches and clocks. We are romantics. We want time to fit in with our moods. It should be drinking time when we feel like a drink, and sleeping time when we feel like sleeping. How is the Englishman to understand that? He's been a clock-watcher since the day he was born. Do you know, English mothers even feed their babies and put them to bed according to the clock? (162)

With the help of this passage, Anita Desai has properly compared two different cultures—Oriental and Occidental. The Orientals do not believe too much in watches, whereas the Occidentals are too punctual in their visiting hours and prompt in doing their work. As Adit says that Orientals are romantics who believe in mood rather than timings. By supplementing some factual examples, Adit appreciates the good habits of the Occidentals who live their lives in accordance with a clock. On the contrary, he passes negative remarks on the Orientals who consider no time constraint. Here the comparison of two cultures is not important, but cultural differences should be considered positively for maintaining social health and strength. After all, there is no one culture, which is perfect, but each culture has something novel to share. Multiculturalism not only supports cultural pluralism but also respects uniqueness and distinctiveness of each culture. Therefore, cultural clashes have no place on the agenda of multiculturalism. The present analytical study of this novel simply shows how multiculturalism functions in different forms to resolve some socio-cultural problems that create waves of friction and hostility in the world.

5

Multiculturalism in *The God of Small Things*

India is a vast multicultural and heavily populated country with noteworthy social, economic and religious disparities. India's constitution is a basic document of Indian multiculturalism that recognizes cultural, religious and gender equality. But despite new legal formulations, cultural, religious and gender discriminations continue to impose serious and considerable restrictions, especially on women and untouchables.

Kerala is a multicultural and multireligious state. Until recently it was stratified on the basis of caste, class and gender. Caste system in Kerala was so rigid and its rigidity has created different social problems. Swami Vivekananda was shocked by the rigidity of the caste discrimination in Kerala and said it had made the state a 'madhouse'. Of course, the communist rule in the state has improved the condition of the dalits and the working class considerably. And presently casteism is not a visible evil, yet it has spread itself into the politics, religion, and society of Kerala. Caste is one of the deciding factors, which also controls the political strategies in the state. Thus, at the practical level, caste system has become a major hurdle in implementing a multicultural policy in Kerala. One of the apparent indications of the Hindu influence in Kerala is the prevalence and importance of the caste system. It is generally said that caste was originally present only in 'Hinduism', but it has been a subject of consideration for other religions also.

Caste has now become more of a social phenomenon than a religious convention in Kerala. The extreme importance of caste system is seen in the upper caste Syrian Christian and Brahmin communities in Kerala. However, class is also a form of social stratification, though it is quite different from caste. Class is based on the possession of economic status or the division of society into unequal strata or groups. In Kerala, high caste people enjoy more wealth and opportunities than the low caste people who perform menial jobs. Among the low caste people, untouchables (dalits) have the lowest standing and usually the lowest economic position. Though multiculturalism embodies the principles of equality, freedom, justice and human dignity, the so-called upper caste people in Kerala bluntly violate all these principles and control the power structure of the society. Such blunt violations may not always be very explicit, but their subtle presence is felt in every walk of Kerala life. Gender discrimination is also a vicious tendency which causes numerous problems to the 'second sex'. From the ancient period, Kerala society has been prejudiced against the female gender although the matriarchal system in some Hindu sects has had its positive results. The male dominated society often single-handedly deals with the entire social, religious, cultural and family affairs, without much feminine consideration. Due to this dominant patriarchal culture, especially in non-Hindu communities, Kerala women had not got enough chance to grow independently as self-reliant people. They were only custodians of cultural values and social norms imposed by the dominant patriarchal culture. It is often said that a woman needs protection and patronage at every stage of her life because of the secondary status accorded to her in society. In Kerala, the dominant patriarchal culture controls women in such a way that they have no other choice than to surrender themselves to certain patriarchal values. Because of the man-made rigid social structure and patriarchal ideologies, the male always dominates and dictates terms to women—sometimes by force and sometimes by praise. As N. Andal (2002: 29) views: "Though the Indian woman has come a long way in her cultural level from the vedic period to the present status of achieving economic independence in the

21 century, yet due to many social, religious, cultural and political demands on her, she is still bound by the shackles of certain traditions and rituals, which distort her image to all around her." The Kerala woman's case is no exception.

Thus, gender equality and recognition of differences in terms of identity do not seem to be the basic principles of Indian multiculturalism. Legally, men and women are considered to be equals but socially, culturally and economically women are not free to enjoy their lives due to the dominant patriarchal culture and social taboos. Hence, a remarkable aspect of post-colonial creative writing in English has been the author's pre-occupation with the issues related to women and the downtrodden.

In Kerala, people from different castes, communities and religions have been living together but they do not seem to have internalized the principles of multiculturalism, i.e. 'different but equal', because of traditional and conventional ways of life. Caste/class antagonism, gender discrimination and imposition of patriarchal culture are still genuine problems, which are being exposed and highlighted in the novel *The God of Small Things*. The narrative of the novel centers around the Ayemenem house, in which tradition and history shape the lives of its inhabitants who have been blindly following the dead conventions, rigid value systems and age-old rules. The late Reverend E. John Ipe, the oldest member of the family, had started a school for untouchables. Indeed, the establishment of the school is a positive sign of social equality and equal opportunity to all castes and communities. But he was a caste conscious old-timer who was insisting his family members to obey the rules of family and its traditional value system. He was always conscious of his family's reputation and the concepts of love and sexual morality. As a representative of the dominant patriarchal culture, Reverend Ipe was always trying to pressurize/control the female members in the family. His wife, Aleyooty Ammachi, was an early victim of the patriarchal culture. Her submissiveness and dissatisfaction are clearly suggested in one of the portraits hung on the wall of the Ayemenem house:

> Aleyooty Ammachi looked more hesitant. As though she would have liked to turn around but couldn't. Perhaps it wasn't as easy for her to abandon the river. With her eyes she looked in the direction that her husband looked. With her heart she looked away. (30)

The description of their portrait shows how Ammachi's life was mortgaged to the dominant patriarchal culture, a basic agency of female oppression, exploitation and marginalisation. In fact, she wanted to see the beauty of the world through her eyes, but she couldn't move her eyes because of her husband's moral rigidity. This portrait silently explains how patriarchy has controlled and imposed its rules on the women in Ayemenem house.

Reverend Ipe's son, Pappachi, in spite of his cosmopolitan, rational and 'scientific' life outside Kerala is a worthy successor to his father. He imposes himself upon the female members of the family and restricts their lives. The women in the Ayemenem house are not so free, because of male domination. Pappachi, the present head of the family, always thinks about family's 'reputation' and preserves the discriminatory values, which give rise to the rebellious spirit of Ammu. Due to male hypocrisy, vanity and brutishness, Ammu starts developing her rebellious spirit and shatters the values that the Ayemenem house has been cherishing for many many decades.

Ammu is not the only single female character in the Ayemenem house who is harassed and exploited by its male chauvinists. Her mother, Mammachi, is also a victim of male domination. Mammachi's entomologist husband, Pappachi, harasses her mentally and physically: "Every night he beats her with a brass flower vase. The beatings weren't new. What was new was only the frequency with which they took place." (47-48)

But as a representative of the old generation, she bears her husband's male chauvinism and brutality. Though Pappachi beats her ruthlessly, she tolerates him and avoids clashes in the family. As a silent sufferer, she seems to believe in male chauvinism and never raises a finger against his vindictiveness. Both Ammu and her mother are the victims of mental and physical degradation inflicted on them by the males of the family. But Mammachi submits herself to the patriarchal values, whereas Ammu rebels against the patriarchy. The root cause of mental as well physical harassment is perhaps located in the unequal balance of power between men and women. Dominant patriarchal culture assigns low value to women and girls which result in their harassment and exploitation. The overall denials of equal rights to women through cultural and social norms reinforce violence against them. It is said that non-recognition is a form of oppression. Indian patriarchal culture doesn't recognize female identity, because of its age-old traditional misconceptions about male-female relations. Gender identity is socially embedded, whereas sexual identity is biological. Mammachi represents the old generation whereas Ammu is a representative of the new generation. Mammachi's passivity is a sign of changelessness of patriarchal ideologies but Ammu's rebellious spirit inaugurates a feminist move towards equal rights and respect to all irrespective of their caste, class, gender and community.

Chacko, another patriarchal voice in the Ayemenem house, enjoys all privileges, which are deliberately denied to his sister, Ammu. Chacko sexually exploits the women workers in his pickle factory and his mother, Mammachi, a capitalist, exploits them economically. Mother and son are aware of each other's line of exploitation. Mammachi silently permits Chacko to have sexual relations with women workers. She even slips them money:

> She secretly slipped them money to keep them happy. They took it because they needed it. They had young children and old parents. Or husbands who spent all their earnings in toddy bars. (169)

Her silence speaks a lot about her hypocrisy. Ironically, Chacko is a self-proclaimed Marxist who is expected to protect the rights of workers but he calls pretty working women to his room on the pretext of teaching them labour rights and trade union laws. He pretends to be a Comrade, a preacher of equality, but in reality he is a lecher, a vile manipulator of women.

Chacko's sexual harassment of women workers in the factory is a common practice, but nobody objects to it, because he is a member of the dominant Syrian Christian class. Due to poverty, women workers silently and passively tolerate Chacko's sexual harassment. Simultaneously, as a member of the dominant patriarchal culture, Chacko harasses his sister, Ammu, when she violates the love laws of the Ayemenem house. From a feminist perspective, it is significant that the 'Love Laws' of the family are not equally applicable to all its members. Though Mammachi is fully aware of her son's illicit relations with women, she is unperturbed. In fact, she gets a back door built for Chacko to enter in and meet his 'man's needs':

> Mammachi had a separate entrance built for Chacko's room, which was at the eastern end of the house, so that the objects of his 'needs' wouldn't have to go traipsing through the house. (169)

As mentioned earlier, Mammachi encourages her son's illicit relations by paying money to the women workers. But when it comes to Ammu, her own daughter, she applies a different set of love laws, a kind of double standard. Ammu is a victim of dead conventions and rigid rules where gender discrimination is one of the common issues on the hidden agenda of a patriarchal household. It obviously shows that the mode of application of rules differs from gender to gender and class to class. In a sense, the so-called feudal protectors of the social norms socially and culturally accept Chacko's sexual sovereignty. So, as a representative of an elite/dominant culture, he is exempted from the normal love laws. As Rama Kundu (2001: 174) says: "Ammu had been humiliated and cornered by her father, ill-treated and betrayed by her husband, insulted by the police, rendered destitute by her brother; each of them voiced the patriarchal ideology which commanded that 'she' should have no individual rights anywhere-as daughter/wife/citizen/sister—but should rather be an object, preferably submissive."

Ammu's insignificant presence in the family and society forces her to go against the dominant patriarchal culture, which blocks her way to liberty and freedom. Human society is an amalgamation of differences existing in terms of status, interest, talent and opinions, because heterogeneity and diversity are facts of human life. Whatever steps Ammu has taken against the patriarchal culture needs to be considered as a consequence of her interest and need. But she wants to cross the boundaries of caste, community and culture for developing a new version of multiculturalism. Chacko, a custodian of the patriarchal culture, tortures Ammu. When he comes to know about her relations with Velutha, he threatens her: "Get out of my house before I break every bone in your body!" (225). This utterance reveals Chacko's anti-women attitude and his faith in the values of old patriarchy.

Arundhati Roy's protest in *The God of Small Things* stems from her sense of outrage at the slave-like status of women in free democratic India. Indeed the marginalisation of women is a global phenomenon, but the degree of marginalisation differs from place to place. Arundhati Roy in the novel attempts to offer a set of directions to change the status of women in Indian society. She seems to support a rebellious perspective to establish a radical feminine identity in India. So, *The God of Small Things* is not only a story of the Ipe family but also of the disempowered sections of Indian society.

The Ayemenem house is a place where the evils of oppression, exploitation and injustice reign over a group of helpless women. Mammachi, Baby Kochamma, Ammu and Rahel are members representing different generations, but without exception, they have all received ill-treatment and the shocks of humiliation from the brutal patriarchal culture of the family and a vicious social structure.

Baby Kochamma's position in Ayemenem house is neither prestigious nor assertive. She simply gloats over the name and reputation of the Ipe family. But her words and actions reveal her prejudice against caste, colour and class. She is very conscious of Ammu's strange behaviour in and outside the house. When she mutters about Ammu-Velutha affair, she conveniently forgets her past. She has violated the love rules of the house dictated by its male members. At the age of eighteen, she fell in love with Father Mulligan, an Irish monk. She attempted to seduce Father Mulligan with weekly exhibitions of staged charity but she couldn't get any response from him. Undaunted, she went on playing different tricks to trap him. Asking some irrelevant questions was one such trick:

> There's something I wanted to ask you, Father, Baby Kochamma would say. 'In First Corinthians, chapter ten, verse twenty-three, it says.... "All things are lawful for me, but all things are not expedient". Father, how can all things be lawful unto Him? I mean I can understand if some things are lawful for Him, but—' (23).

This exposes her strong desire to launch an affair with Father Mulligan. But very soon she realizes the futility of her efforts. Baby Kochamma's approach was foolishly covert. When all her attempts at creating a love affair fail, she submits herself to the standards of the house, which are blatantly inhuman and destructive. Thus, out of jealousy, she misrepresents the Ammu-Velutha affair at the Kottayam Police Station. The whole family joins hands against Ammu, each member hiding his/her own sexual exploitation and misadventures. The pride, envy and caste consciousness of the Ayemenem house are reflected in the character of Baby Kochamma who lives her 'backward' life. Hiding her own sexual weakness, failure and egotism and indulging in self-righteousness, she humiliates and troubles Ammu and her children:

> Baby Kochamma disliked the twins, for she considered them doomed, fatherless waifs. Worse still, they were Half-Hindu Hybrids whom no self respecting Syrian Christian would ever marry. She was keen for them to realize that they (like herself) lived on sufferance in the Ayemenem house...where they really had no right to be. Baby Kochamma resented Ammu, because she saw her quarrelling with a fate that she, Baby Kochamma herself, felt she had graciously accepted. The fate of the wretched Man-less woman...she had managed to persuade herself over the years that her unconsummated love for Father Mulligan had been entirely due to her

> restraint and her determination to do the right thing. (45)

In her self-righteous mood Baby Kochamma thinks she has done the right thing accept her fate. She is jealous of Ammu because Ammu does not accept her fate, she rather challenges it. In spite of her 'wrongdoing' Ammu has the satisfaction that she is not yielding to the laws of the family. Baby Kochamma cannot admire the courage of Ammu, although she could have been successful if she had not enslaved herself to the family's value system.

The Ayemenem house keeps reminding its members, with brutal force, that it is dangerous to rise against its tradition, conventions, culture and love rules. The older members of the house are more conservative and they have nurtured their brutishness, pretense, egotism, male chauvinism and sexual jealously. In this regard, Simon G. Bernabas (1999: 302) views: "Sexual jealousy, gender discrimination, foolish dependence on the colonial legacy, cruelty, discriminary caste feelings and callousness are character traits found in most members of the Ayemenem House." Thus, the Ayemenem house stands for moral decadence. It maintains hypocritical admiration of old value system which spoils the lives of the women folk and the weak.

The God of Small Things is essentially the story of men and women who have been neglected at the 'margins' of society and have to pay a heavy price for being born either an untouchable or a woman. Ammu, the heroine of the novel, is a representative character in a typical patriarchal society. From the beginning, she gets no chance to bloom and grow independently due to social, cultural and religious interferences. Ammu is shown throughout the novel as conscious not only of her sexuality, but of her emotional needs. But as a subordinate and marginalized woman she is not allowed to pursue her studies, because of the perverted patriarchal notions against women's education. Indeed, multiculturalism demands equal opportunities for all cultures, castes, communities and genders. But Ammu gets no chance to continue her education like her brother, Chacko, who enjoys all the privileges within and outside the family. He has had the opportunity to study abroad. Here, the principle of equal opportunity has been violated by the dominant patriarchal culture. It is her own father, Pappachi, who violates the principle of equal opportunity and deprives Ammu of higher education. In spite of his scientific temper and stay abroad, he continues to be a typical orthodox Syrian Christian patriarch whose idea is that "a college education was an unnecessary expense for a girl" (38).

Pappachi's prejudice against her education shows his general prejudice against the second sex. He is unwilling to accept her female identity and her right to education. Ammu is a representative of the minority culture whose voice has been stifled by a dominant patriarchal culture. Denying higher education to Ammu is a sign of sidetracking 'the second sex' from her basic human rights. In fact, all cultures are valuable, but the validity and authenticity of each culture depends on how much that culture protects and projects the basic human rights, irrespective of gender, caste and class. As a woman, Ammu becomes the victim of injustice, exclusion, marginalisation, dispossession and gender discrimination, because the male oppressors within her family and the society blindly maintain the dead conventions and state moral values without any human considerations. The social activist in Roy seems to argue that non-recognition of minority cultures, denial of the basic human rights of women and gender discrimination are still basic (pending) issues in postmodern India.

On the other hand, Chacko, Ammu's brother, enjoys all privileges and advantages in the family and also gets a chance to go to Oxford to pursue his higher studies. This double standard of patriarchal hegemony reveals the prejudice against the second sex. Ammu is a deprived daughter in her father's house. Pappachi neglects her and makes no provision for her marriage. Being a father, Pappachi escapes from his fatherly duty of seeking marriage proposals for his daughter. Roy thus demonstrates the biased patriarchal mentality, which deliberately promotes the politics of difference in gender and derecognizes minority cultures. Though acknowledging of differences is one of the principles of multiculturalism, in the novel. Gender, caste, culture and religious differences are used for unmasking the male dominated society's craze for marginalization and exclusion.

Ammu is badly exploited and harassed by the man-made social institutions and the power structure of Indian society. Upto a certain limit, she remains passive but eventually she emerges as a rebel who challenges not only the oppressive patriarchal culture but also the brutal forces of social institutions.

As a female child, she has no space in her family. From the beginning, she has been mentally harassed and physically tortured by her own father. At the age of eighteen, she becomes more desperate, because of her father's negligence. Hence, she tries to escape from the loveless Ayemenem house to Calcutta for a temporary relief: "She thought that 'anything', anyone at all, would be better than returning to Ayemenem" (39).

At a Bengali wedding reception, she meets a youth and loses her heart to him and marries him without informing her parents. This independent decision of engaging in an intercommunity love marriage marks the beginning of her rebellion against the dictatorial patriarchal culture of her family. Ammu, a member of the upper class Syrian Christian community, breaks the patriarchal rules of matrimony and the false traditional value systems of her own family and makes an earnest attempt to develop her own female identity. However, her entirely personal decision creates grave problems for her. The members of her family start looking at her as a menace to their cultural, traditional and community rules. Ammu has dared to marry outside her community without her parents' consent and her act apparently has brought 'disgrace' and 'dishonor' to the family.

In a sense, Ammu's intercommunity love marriage is her way of understanding cultural pluralism and regional differences. But the mainstream culture is hostile to her and it doesn't accommodate other cultures because of its prejudice against them. Yet Ammu's daring suggests the possibility of establishing genuine love across geographical and cultural boundaries.

As a social ideology, multiculturalism welcomes cultural diversity and accepts internal plurality of all cultures. But in the novel, the mainstream culture, i.e. the culture of the Syrian Christians is not so flexible as to accommodate the minority cultures. After all, any social institution like marriage or religion is the basic source of cultural transmission. Ammu's intercommunity love marriage is a right step to bridge the gap between cultures and communities. But the mainstream culture is not ready to recognize and accommodate other distinctive cultures. After her marriage, she tries to change her 'imprisoned' life and her 'rebellious' spirit challenges; the traditional values that are so partial, inhuman and brutish. Her changed appearance and habits bring out the rebel in her: "She wore backless blouses with her saris and carried a silver lame purse on a chain. She smoked cigarettes in a silver cigarette holder and learned to blow perfect smoke rings." (40)

But very soon, she runs into grave problems in her married life. She realizes that her alcoholic Bengali husband is no better than the Ayemenem males. He too harasses her mentally and physically and tries to push her into the hands of Mr. Hollick, his boss, to be sexually exploited. Roy uses this situation to suggest the white colonizers' tendency to win their male employees for personal sexual misadventures with the latter's wives. Mr. Hollick, a lecherous man, indirectly expresses to Ammu's husband his sexual attraction for Ammu:

> You're very lucky man, you know, wonderful family, beautiful children, such an attractive wife.... He lit a cigarette, and allowed the match to burn until he couldn't hold it any more. 'An extremely attractive wife....' (42)

Perhaps what is worse is Ammu's husband's slavish dependence on the boss and his readiness to fulfill his employer's indirect sexual demands. Thus, he forces her to accept his boss's sexual demand. But she bluntly refuses to be a sexual object for Mr. Hollick, although her husband attacks her physically: "Suddenly he lunged at her, grabbed her hair, punched her and then passed out from the effort" (42).

Ammu's physical exploitation by her husband indicates the typical Indian male's inherited assumption of superiority. However, Roy deftly portrays Ammu's growth as a rebel and the latter's determination to challenge all kinds of male domination:

> Ammu took down the heaviest book she could find in the book-shelf. The Reader's Digest World Atlas—and hit him with it as hard as she could. On his head. His legs. His back and shoulders. When he regained consciousness, he was puzzled by his bruises. (42)

Ammu's reaction indicates the gradual ascension of her rebellious spirit against the hegemonic 'male' culture, which damages lives of innocent women. Ammu has been a close observer of her family's perverted ideologies. In fact, she has been a dormant rebel from the beginning. And when the rebel begins to act, many age-old institutions also suffer setbacks. Continuous physical exploitation makes her leave her alcoholic husband who has been treating her as a commodity. Ammu's decision to separate herself from her husband should be considered as the growth of her rebellious spirit. However, very soon the speed of her rebellious spirit gets checked for some time. Now, having nobody to lean on, Ammu has no other option than to go back to Ayemenem. Her arrival at her parents' house, with her twins, disturbs all family members: "Ammu left her husband and returned unwelcomed, to her parents in Ayemenem. To everything she had fled from only a few years ago. Except now she had two children. And no more dreams" (42).

Ammu's unwelcome return to Ayemenem house offers the members of the family and society a chance to subdue her. Indian society sometimes accepts widowhood graciously, but not a divorced girl, who has no status either in her parents' house or in the society. Male domination within her family and social prejudice against a divorcee pushes Ammu into the pit of isolation, suffering and distress.

At her parents' house, Ammu's mental suffering increases day by day. As a marginalized being, she is restless. Nobody sympathizes with her because in the eyes of the members of her family, she is a divorcee, a status she has secured for herself by violating the 'love laws' of Ayemenem house. The local people also start avoiding her and this also keeps her in isolation with her shattered dreams and innocent twins. Her own parents neglect her and insult her on different occasions. These instances of mental harassment by her parents and society develop a sense of alienation in Ammu. It is obvious that her unusual marriage and divorce are treated by her own people as the causes of her mental harassment. At a personal level, she has the burden of singly-handedly bring up her children who for others are like millstone around her neck. At the social level, she has been cornered as an 'outcaste'. She realizes that she has only a marginalized existence in the house. Any other woman in her position could have accepted the ignominious existence as fate. But Ammu's spirit becomes stronger when the pressure of domination weighs down on her. The revolt that she holds within herself had to be borne with pain because of her knowledge that she and her kids are parasites at her own house. Hence, for a time, she bears the insults of her brother and the vicious remarks of the local moralists. Ammu, being a divorcee and mother of two children, has no "Locus Standi" in the society. Such marginalisation is sufficient for her to form for herself a philosophy of life that varies considerably from the seemingly moral philosophy of the Ayemenem house. The unusual philosophy that she gradually formulates for herself is the outcome of such bold actions: "She spent hours on the riverbank with her little plastic transistor shaped like a tangerine. She smoked cigarettes and had midnight swims." (44)

Her strange behaviour is one of the signs of her growing rebellious spirit against the dominant patriarchal culture which disregards and ignores her. According to Tapan Kumar Ghosh (1999: 191): "The revolt of Ammu is against patriarchy, against the calculated torture and hypocrisy of the male-chauvinist society. She struggles not only against history but also to be woman to attain her feminine fulfillment which is denied by males, proletariat (Pillai) and bourgeois (Pappachi and Chacko) alike."

The revolt attains denser manifestations: "She wore flowers in her hair and carried magic secrets in her eyes. She spoke to no one" (44). Nobody can fathom the depth of her eyes and silence. In fact her silence speaks a lot about her 'lost' female identity. As we know, the word 'identity' is very slippery because it is multidimensional. Literally, both 'identity' and 'self' mean the same, but in cultural theory, identity is used to describe the consciousness of the self in a modern individual. The modern individual is quite autonomous and self-reliant who boldly challenges the orthodoxy and creates a space for his/her own identity. In a multicultural country like India, identity recognition is one of the most important principles of promoting the ideology of multiculturalism. But in Ammu's case, instead of recognizing her female identity, people start plotting against her. And the plotting is essentially a consequence of Ammu's 'wrong' choice of a husband. But, perhaps more than anyone else in her family, she has great respect for marriage and especially for the identities of her children. She seems to endorse Simon de Beauvoir's (1961: 62) view of married life: "Marriage is not only an honorable career and one less tiring than many others: it alone permits a woman to keep her social dignity intact and at the same time to find sexual fulfillment as loved one and mother...." In marrying a Bengali, she is seeking, like any other woman, social dignity and the right to fulfill her sexual needs. But Ammu's marriage gets no social sanction because her family has warped and outdated notions of marriage and its laws. The notions find a clear expression in these words of Baby Kochamma:

> She subscribed wholeheartedly to the commonly held view that a married daughter had no position in her parents' home. As for a divorced daughter—according to Baby Kochamma, she had no position anywhere at all. And as for a divorced daughter from a love marriage, well, words could not describe Baby Kochamma's

> outrage. As for a divorced daughter from an intercommunity love marriage—Baby Kochamma chose to remain quiveringly silent on the subject. (45-46)

Liberal feminists always fight for existing social prejudice against women. They claim that women should have the same rights and the opportunities as men. Due to their subordinate position in society, women suffer a lot in terms of economic, social, cultural and religious rights. So gender discrimination needs to be acknowledged for promoting a common culture and equality among the sexes. The idea of gender difference is very much central to contemporary feminism and the discourse on multiculturalism also speaks about the principle of differences—may be gender, cultural, religious or ethnic and recommends the accommodation of all those differences. It means, at certain levels, both feminism and multiculturalism speak commonly for respecting 'differences'. So instead of imposing a set of man-made rules of the dominant culture, women should be allowed to grow independently in society. This is precisely what Arundhati Roy attempts to do by gradually developing the spirit of revolt in her character, Ammu.

Though Mammachi and Baby Kochamma are her close relatives, they are not sympathetic to Ammu and her innocent children. Roy's point is that even in a literate society like Kerala, women's suffering at the hands of family and society does not vary considerably. Patriarchy is a curse in Kerala as it is elsewhere. So is women's suffering inflicted on them by members of their own gender?

Ammu's sense of revolt takes a concrete shape from the time she sees Velutha. It is significant that Roy makes Ammu get attracted to a dalit for whom the Ayemenem house has no respect at all. Not that Ammu cannot find a Syrian Christian lover in Ayemenem. But, Roy seems to believe, he will be no different from Chacko, the sexual hypocrite. Roy takes Ammu to the raw, natural man who can be more original and sincere in love than the so-called civilized men of Ayemenem. Velutha is ready to suffer for his love. He, too, like Ammu, is capable of violating the age-old laws which forbid genuine man-woman relationships. Like her, again, he too is dispossessed and marginalized. In one of their earliest chance meetings, they both realize that they are made for each other, that they are beyond all man-made love laws, and that the history that existed before the formation of these laws has been waiting for their union. See the impact of just one look at each other:

> The man standing in the shade of the rubber tree with coins of sunshine dancing on his body, holding her daughter in his arms glanced up and caught Ammu's gaze. Centuries telescoped into one evanescent moment. History was wrong-footed, caught off guard. Sloughed off like an old snakeskin. Its marks, its scars, its wounds from old wars and the walking backwards days all fell away. In its left an aura, a palpable shimmering that was as plain to see as the water in a river or the sun in the sky. As plain to feel as the heat on a hot day, or the tug of a fish on a taut line. So obvious that no one noticed.
>
> In that brief moment, Velutha looked up and saw things that he hadn't seen before. Things that had been out of bounds so far, obscured by history's blinkers.
>
> Simple things.
>
> For instance, he saw that Rahel's mother was a woman.
>
> That she had deep dimples when she smiled and that they stayed on long after her smile left her eyes. He saw that her brown arms were round and firm and perfect. That her shoulders shone, but her eyes were somewhere else. He saw that when he gave her gifts they no longer needed to be offered flat on the palms of his hands so that she wouldn't have to touch him. His boats and boxes. His little windmills. He saw too that he was not necessarily the only giver of gifts. That she had gifts to give him too.
>
> This knowing slid into him cleanly, like the sharp edge of a knife. Cold and hot at once. It only took a moment.
>
> Ammu saw that he saw. She looked away. He did too. History's fiends returned to claim them. To rewrap them

> in its old, scarred pelt and drag them back to where they really lived. (176-77)

And now Ammu can think beyond culture, caste and community barriers. A sexually deprived and mentally harassed woman, she allows her rebellious spirit to unfold itself by drifting towards Velutha, a man with 'man's body', and thus break the age-old, tyrannical rules of love. Ammu's rebellious spirit disturbs the so-called defenders of the love laws: "It was a time when the unthinkable became thinkable and the impossible really happened" (31).

Ammu, the 'Unmixable Mix', with her trodden youth, oppressed existence and frustrated dreams, drifts towards another representative of the oppressed and marginalized class, Velutha, and decides to obtain solace in his arms. Umed Singh (2006: 89) says: "They transgress the Love Laws and establish physical relationship with each other. They seek solace in each other's arms because they belong to the same 'class' i.e. marginalized and oppressed class."

Yet the civilization and the love laws that Ammu and Velutha decide to challenge are too strong for them. The history of that civilization is the history of oppression and murder. It has spared hardly anyone challenger. Ammu and Velutha can be no exception, although their effort is to establish an original multicultural living in the face of the opposition of a false civilization that promotes a false multiculturalism. The 'unholy' and 'unequal' alliance between Ammu and Velutha cost them their lives. Her parents start harassing her mentally. Velutha is treacherously arrested and tortured to death in the police station. When Ammu comes to know about Velutha's arrest, immediately she rushes to the police station, where the Police Inspector Thomas Mathew humiliates her. Roy describes the humiliating scene thus:

> He stared at Ammu's breasts as he spoke. He said the police knew all they needed to know and that the Kottayam police didn't take statement from 'veshya' or their illegitimate children. (8)

Though Inspector Thomas Mathew is a custodian of law and order, he bluntly denies Ammu's statement and calls her a 'veshya'. He stares lustfully at her breasts. Nobody spares Ammu; even Comrade Pillai, an opportunist from the Marxist camp, insults her because of her act of breaking the rules of love, which are made and controlled by the so-called dominant patriarchal society. Different forces like judiciary, patriarchy and politics meet to punish Ammu and Velutha, the 'rebels', who have formed their own rules of love.

After Velutha's tragic death, Ammu is forced to leave Ayemenem house because the Velutha incident coincided with Sophie Mol's death. The last phase of Ammu's life reveals the brutal force of her antagonists:

> Ammu died in a grimy room in the Bharat Lodge in Alleppey, where she had gone for a job interview as someone's secretary. She died alone. With a noisyceiling fan for company and no Estha to lie at the back of her and talk to her. She was thirty-one. Not old, not young, but a viable, die-able age. (161)

As a 'sinner' Ammu is made to suffer in all possible ways and she dies anonymously, just a receipt number, with nobody even to shed a drop of tear for her, not even her own daughter Rahel. Ammu's suffering does not end with her death. The church now plays its role by refusing to burry her. In brief, Ammu is not the victim of a single force, but forces like an old value system, patriarchy, caste/class antagonism, gender discrimination, culture, religion, politics, judiciary and especially her blood relatives. Ammu remains a 'name' registered in the book of Ayemenem history:

> Would future generations say, 'There was Ammu-Ammu Ipe. Married a Bengali. Went quite mad. Died young. In a cheap lodge somewhere. (223)

Indeed the vicious agencies of history—such as family, judiciary, politics and religion succeed in eliminating Velutha and Ammu. Yet Roy treats them with dignity, for they are people who make an attempt to establish a subculture that has its roots in love. By sacrificing their own lives they are trying to see whether such a natural love relationship can survive in an advancing civilization. Roy, by depicting their death, highlights the vicious strength of the so-called civilized society. It is a society that can violate all norms of love: "They all broke the rules. They all crossed into forbidden territory. They all tampered with the laws that lay down who should be loved and how. And how much" (31).

Ammu's natural but socially unacceptable relationship causes a series of events that change the lives of her twins, Estha and Rahel. Ammu is the central antagonist in the struggle against the established rules of love. When she realizes her affection for Velutha, she doesn't hesitate to enter into the forbidden territories of love. But her act of breaking society's rules of love that her own people react against her rather brutally. However, for the realization of her self she needs to bear the reaction. Ignoring social restrictions, caste and class barriers, both Ammu and Velutha come together and form their own rules of 'love', which are more 'human' and sincere than the laws made by the members of her own family and society.

As breakers of 'Love Laws', both have made an attempt to develop their own 'way of life', i.e. their 'subculture'. But the proponents and the so-called custodians of the dominant culture never allow the emergence of such a 'subculture'. Indeed each subculture has its different beliefs, perceptions and various ways of thinking, feeling, but here the emerging subculture doesn't grow independently. Their attempt of shaping the subculture gains no wider acceptance due to the pressure of the dominant mainstream culture. Their subculture is diametrically opposed to the mainstream culture which is deeply rooted in its age-old tradition. The new emerging subculture has no mechanism of its own for social acceptance. According to Nazma Malik (1999: 164): "There is no one culture; India comprises of a number of subcultures which have distinct position in the Indian social ethos. All these subcultures have a right to exist as Indians." However, a subculture exhibits its distinctive character and structure but in the case of Ammu and Velutha, the mainstream culture supersedes the subculture they try to create for themselves. There are different types of subcultures, but Ammu and Velutha have tried to develop a radical subculture to resist the dominant love norms of the mainstream culture. And that causes their destruction.

Yet Roy does not seem to be pessimistic; nor does she seem to think that the death of Ammu and Velutha has put an end to the efforts of the marginalized to form a society where human beings of various cultures and background can live together, without sacrificing their cultural identity. Oppressive dominant cultures will have to face the challenges of more Veluthas and Ammus. As their number increases, there is every likelihood of the weakening of the merciless hold of the mainstream cultures.

Indeed the biology of sex is a powerful factor that causes physical attraction between Ammu and Velutha. The vivid description of their physique underlines their love for each other's body. But Roy does not seem to think that love is sinful. The members of Ayemenem family have been victims of that passion. Chacko's lust for the working class women is not essentially different from Ammu's love for Velutha. In fact, Ammu is more sincere, for she is with Velutha even at the police station, whereas Chacko's love, nurtured by his own mother, is based on his money power and it is sheer exploitation of helpless women workers. So Ammu's love is not purely physical although attraction for the body has its role to play. She can have safe sex with the members of her own community. But her purpose is revolt which is against a fake culture and as such its impact should be shocking. It is an effort to establish a multiculturalism that transcends all man-made boundaries and restrictions.

Roy has also demonstrated the universal fact about human biology that there are no taboos and cultural traits in the question of sex and love. Ammu and Velutha have followed the natural and universal laws of human biology, which their subculture intends to celebrate. Man made love cultures have no place before the universal laws, because cultural values regarding human love need to be realistic and true. Ammu and

Velutha have accepted each other on the basis of mutual trust and love; they understand their common disadvantages of being a woman and an outcaste. This understanding is valuable to them. Ammu and Velutha share a lot of common things, because both are in a sense 'untouchables' who are wounded by caste, gender, community and class barriers. Indeed every member of Ayemenem house more or less secretly violated these universal laws of sex but Ammu wants to legitimize the laws in the subculture she is trying to establish with Velutha. Both Ammu and Velutha belong to the same class, i.e. the oppressed class, and both have 'gifts' to give each other: "He saw too that he was not necessarily the only giver of gifts. That she had gifts to give him too" (176-77).

Ammu, a challenger of social taboos, breaks the rules of love not only for her own sake but for the sake of her lovable twins, who are left uncared for and unloved in Ayemenem house. Her motherly affection is the best sign of her feminine culture but all the blind followers of mainstream culture are against her due to the age-old misconceptions and misinterpretations of the term 'culture' which they have accepted for discriminating people on the ground of gender, caste and class. After all, culture is to be understood as something that is owned by all people in different ways. It is very dynamic and progressive and not the property of a particular group, gender or caste. So there is no point in glorifying any specific culture, because every culture has its own flavor and color, which reflect the individual's ways of thinking, talking and feeling. In a sense, the attempt of Ammu and Velutha to establish a natural subculture is neither anti-social nor anti-cultural but it is quite instinctive and innate. Imposing too many restrictions on healthy instincts can lead to personal and social tragedies. And that is what has happened in their case.

Roy further demonstrates that, though the law of human biology acts uniformly and universally, irrespective of caste and class, the dominant culture has used sex as a means to exploit women and the weaker cultures/classes. Roy is showing in Velutha-Ammu relationship the consequences of reversing human biology by a 'low' class man and an upper caste woman. She also wants to emphasize the fact that sex can cross barriers but if it is between two disparate classes there can be dangerous results. Yet she allows their union because Velutha-Ammu relationship has the element of sincerity in it; they wish to stand by each other in the face of all the opposition from the upper class and the society. After each union, they look forward to "Naaley", the next day. Their aim is to explore the possibility of establishing a society where a paravan could lead a married life with a Syrian Christian woman. Indeed, they fail in their attempt, for the forces of society, irrespective of religion and party lines, join hands in polishing them off. Yet, Roy suggests, such forces will have to face more dangerous relationships. Thus at the end of the novel we find sexual relationship progressing to incest between a brother and sister, Estha and Rahel. They go beyond all the hitherto violated laws of love in the family:

> Then she sat up and put her arms around him. Drew him down beside her.
>
> They lay like that for a long time. Awake in the dark. Quietness and Emptiness.
>
> Not old. Not young.
>
> But a viable die-able age.
>
> They were strangers who had met in a chance encounter. They had known each other before Life began.
>
> There is very little that anyone could say to clarify what happened next. Nothing that (in Mammachi's book) would separate Sex from Love. Or Needs from Feelings. (327-28)

Ammu's daughter, Rahel, a representative of the new generation, has also broken the rules of 'Love Laws' and enjoys her 'woman's need' with Estha, her brother. But nobody has taken any objection because from the very beginning, she has been a neglected child having no concern with society and its culture. Comparatively she is freer than her mother because her uncared and unprotected life is not under the control of any culture, tradition, history and social norms. In a sense, Rahel is a completely independent woman who lives her free life according her will and wish. From the very beginning, she is culturally and socially an uprooted girl who doesn't bother about any culture, identity and status. In a real sense individuals like Rahel live their natural life without any man-made rules of society. Rahel's act of violating the rules of love points to a different kind of subculture, which is not similar to the culture her mother has tried to create for herself. She freely enjoys her 'woman's need' with her brother who has been her companion from her birth.

Ammu is punished because of her 'sin' of breaking the 'Love Laws', but her daughter Rahel enjoys her liberal and free life without feeling of any pressure of the dominant culture. It means Rahel succeeds in continuing her mother's failed mission of breaking the boundaries of caste, class and community and the hypocrisy in the name of sex. By breaking the rules of a dominant culture, Rahel proves herself to be an active rebel who revolts against the dominant patriarchal culture and cultivates her new subculture, which is neither dominant nor oppressive but quite natural and human.

Human society needs cultures, which respect all other castes, communities and genders equally. If a mainstream culture is more domineering and partial, Roy seems to argue that some oppressed, marginalized and less privileged groups will join allies to establish their own new subcultures, which may be deviant or opposite. Therefore, the policy of multiculturalism in India promotes equality and justice to all groups and cultures but in this novel, the principles of multiculturalism have been violated to some extent. Multiculturalism is a flexible theory which attempts to promote cultural coexistence and mutual respect to all communities and castes irrespective of their differences and distinctiveness. But in this novel due to caste, class and gender discrimination the 'powerless' have lost their identities to remain passive. The case of Vellaya Pappen, Velutha's father, is an instance of this subjugation.

However, Ammu's version of multiculturalism underlines the fact that a Syrian Christian woman, a member of a dominant culture, can live with Velutha, a Paravan. Though her Bengali husband belongs to the upper caste family, his treatment to Ammu is pitiless and brutish. However, Velutha, a representative of the low caste, has great respect for her and her womanhood.

Roy also portrays the impact of poverty on the dalits. The untouchables have been deprived of their basic right to education because of poverty. In fact, Indian Constitution has given the right to education to all, but even in postmodern India the picture has not changed. The untouchables are still the victims of poverty and social injustice and many remain illiterate. Vellaya Pappen, Velutha's father, could not admit his sons to an English medium school because of poverty and his low social standing. Here, Roy passes her comments on the social discrepancies and barriers that existed in Kerala, where there were separate schools for Touchables and Untouchables.

Due to poverty, Vellaya Pappen could not spare the life of his wife, who was suffering from a chronic disease. His son, Kuttapan, is also a paralytic who cannot get any medical help. Throughout the novel, untouchables are the victims of different forces, may be poverty, tradition, social status, caste, politics, bureaucracy and supremacy of the so-called elites who are basically staunch advocates of oppression, victimization and exploitation. Vellaya Pappen, an old-world Paravan, is always ready to submit himself to the service of the Ayemenem house, because he has been a slave mentally. So he easily gets victimized:

> Velutha's father, Vellaya Pappen, was an old world Paravan. He had seen the Crawling Backwards Days and his gratitude to Mammachi and her family for all that they had done for him, was as wide and deep as a river in spate. (76)

Vellaya Pappen's loyalty with the family is not questionable but his individual identity poses different questions. After all, every person has to maintain his/her individual identity irrespective of his caste, class, culture, community and gender. But Vellaya Pappan always bears in his psyche the burden of the socio-cultural history of Kerala.

Velutha is also victimized by the same social forces, but he tries to maintain his individual identity as a son, carpenter, lover, party leader, friend and a challenger of barriers. Thus, victimization is a socio-cultural problem which can shape a submissive mentality in a person.

Roy poignantly depicts the miserable experiences of Velutha, the untouchable, in *The God of small things*, who transgresses through the means of love the established norms of society. The relationship between Ammu and Velutha is presented as a challenge to the inherited caste system of Indian society. Roy provides us historical information about the scattered dreams of the untouchables who were converted to Christianity. After the arrival of the British to Malabar, a number of low caste people including Velutha's grandfather, Kelan, became Christians in the hope of being freed from the curse of untouchability. But very soon, converted Christians realized that conversion did not improve their social status, because they were discriminated against and treated as the lowest layer within the Christian community. Roy reveals the discriminatory approach of the upper caste Syrian Christians:

> They were made to have separate Churches, with separate services, and separate priests. As a special favour they were even given their own separate Pariah Bishop. (74)

It shows that officially converted low castes were Christians and, theoretically and technically, they enjoyed the rights of the Syrian Christians, but in reality upper caste Christians have not accommodated the converted low caste Christians and have always avoided them by not having any social and marital relations with them. Roy projects this caste antagonism in Kerala where untouchables receive humiliating treatment from the upper caste Hindus and Syrian Christians. The time of the narrative of *The God of Small Things* is 1969, a time when victimization and exploitation of untouchables were still existed in Kerala. Roy presents a lively picture of the untouchables' suffering and the injustice meted out to them. Estha Says:

> In Mammachi's time, Paravans, like other Untouchables, were not allowed to walk on public roads, not allowed to cover their upper bodies, not allowed to carry umbrellas. They had to put their hands over their mouths when they spoke, to divert their polluted breath away from those whom they addressed. (74)

The paravans had a very low status in society and they were not permitted to enter the houses of 'respectable' Syrian Christians in Kerala.

Pappachi, an orthodox Syrian Christian, though highly educated, strictly denies entry to the untouchables: "Pappachi would not allow Paravans into the house. Nobody would. They were not allowed to touch anything that Touchables touched. Caste Hindus and Caste Christians" (73).

This reveals Pappachi's caste preferences. When Baby Kochamma comes to know that Ammu has an intimate sexual relation with Velutha, a Paravan, she is profoundly shocked and expresses her caste and class-consciousness to Mammachi: "How could she stand the smell? Haven't you noticed? They have a particular smell, these Parvans" (257).

Baby Kochamma's remark gives an idea of the intense prejudice and phobia that the upper caste people have against the untouchables. Roy suggests that even though Christianity has survived in India on the strength of low caste converts, these converts have not yet been assimilated into mainstream Christianity. Hence, the relationship between Ammu and Velutha is bound to be doomed. So the caste factor becomes more operative in the Velutha-Ammu affair. When Mammachi comes to know about their relationship, she prepares herself to execute Baby Kochamma's plans against Velutha. According to Mammachi, Velutha's act of having sexual relationship is an indication of the latter's ungratefulness and arrogance.

However, Comrade Pillai, a Marxist leader and a member of the dominant Hindu class, also supports Mammachi and Baby Kochamma in the act of punishing Velutha. When Velutha approaches Pillai for settling his problem, Pillai bluntly refuses his request and informs him that party is not constituted for supporting the workers' indiscipline of their private life. As a professional omletter, Pillai plays a double game. On the one hand, Pillai wants to destroy Velutha's political career, because the latter is emerging in the party as an able worker to be reckoned with. And on the other hand, he wants to play the typical communist politics with the factory 'management' and make personal gains. In the name of caste and class, Pillai tries to play politics and maintains his (chameleon) image as a devoted leader. He retains his caste interest through the agency of his wife and polishes his image to be a casteless and classless leader. As an opportunist, he delivers long speeches before the workers and tries to win their hearts. But his life is that of a petty bourgeois. He always misrepresents Velutha before Chacko and informs him to be cautious about this 'Paravan':

> But frankly speaking, Comrade, Change is one thing. Acceptance is another. You should be cautious. Better for him you send him off.... (279)

Casteism is in the blood of the upper caste people like Pillai. Even the upper caste workers are not ready to accept Velutha's talent only because of his low caste origin. As R.S. Sharma (1998: 63) views: "Arundhati Roy projects class antagonism and class exploitation in terms of caste, and she cleverly makes a contrast between Touchables and Untouchables." Generally upper caste women are too conscious of the superiority of their caste. When Vellaya Pappen approaches Ayemenem house for disclosing an 'undisclosable' news, he is very badly insulted by Mammachi who cannot tolerate the scene being described by him. She starts spitting into the rain and expresses her anger against the subservient and submissive Vellaya Pappen:

> Baby Kochamma, walking past the kitchen, heard the commotion. She found Mammachi spitting into the rain, THOO! THOO! THOO! and Vellaya Pappen lying in the slush, wet, weeping, groveling. Offering to kill his son. To tear him limb from limb. (256)

Roy makes clear the deep rift that exists between Touchables and Untouchables in Kerala, where literacy rate is comparatively higher than that of the other states of India. Moreover, Roy exposes the hypocrisy and duplicity of upper caste people who finally come together to punish Velutha, a Parvan. Even the Police Inspector, Thomas Mathew is against Velutha, because of his low caste origin as a Parvan. Being a custodian of law and order, Thomas Mathew had to protect Velutha, but instead of protecting Velutha, he mercilessly kills him in custody. What is significant here is the fact that all the upper caste people, irrespective of their religion and caste, consider Velutha as a potential threat to their cultural and political identity. Thus, K.N.M. Pillai has no qualms about joining hands with the Syrian Christians to polish off the Parvan, Velutha. Similarly, Inspector Thomas Mathew, a custodian of social justice, is happy to offer 'help' to Baby Kochamma and the Ayemenem house. However, even as they mutually 'help' one another by killing Velutha, there exists between them vicious feelings about their own religions. Thus, although Pillai supports the killing of Velutha, he cannot help Chacko later, when the latter has to close his factory. Seema Bhaduri (1999: 200) views: "In the Velutha-Ammu affair, Roy exposes the conspiracy of caste, class, and political ideologies, each striving to retain its traditional hegemony."

Roy makes an attempt to show the worst mentality of the upper caste/class people who are brutally unjust to those who are from the lower strata of society. The narrative deals with the conflict between individual and society, where the individual fails to resolve the friction between the lower and upper classes in society, because caste always coincides with class and both forces join together to suppress the weaker sections that have already lost their voice before the ages. Roy depicts the character of Velutha, who cannot coexist peacefully with touchables because of the stigma of untouchability attached to him. Velutha, as a reformer in his own way, is trying to explore the possibility of establishing a serious relationship with a touchable woman but the rigid caste and class system cannot subscribe to any such reform and it retaliates so badly that what remains is his 'fractured skull'. It is a fact that caste discrimination in India is a serious social problem. In this respect, J. Bheemaiah (2005: 53) says: "The toe of a Brahmin's shoe was regarded more sacred than the head of a sudra in religious functions." Velutha's head is to be fractured, for he is a possible threat to the caste security of many. Theirs is the fear of civilization: "Civilization's fear of nature, men's fear of women, power's fear of powerlessness" (308). By finishing off Velutha, they are "inoculating a community against an outbreak" (309).

Roy presents a tragic and pessimistic picture of society and expresses her disillusionment with the social conditions of the postcolonial world in which the untouchables are fluttering their (powerless) wings to fly free in the world of humanity, equality and freedom. As a social activist, Roy tries to expose minutely the caste issues but is skeptical about abolishing the caste system. Perhaps, she wants to focus on the reality of Indian society, where the practice of untouchability exists only in the pages of the constitution, but psychologically everyone is conscious of his/her social and religious status. Roy highlights the issue of untouchability and brings to our notice that the stigma of untouchability is still a major problem in India and that it blocks the process of promoting multicultural ideologies based on respect, value and equality to all-caste, community, culture and gender.

Velutha is a man of (communist) vision, self-respect and talent who struggles with Ammu against orthodoxy and casteism. He is in search of the principles of social equality and justice, but gets dejected due to the attached stigma of untouchability. However, he is different from other traditional paravans, because he is a self-made person. As a grown up boy, he starts proving his individual identity as an inventive and imaginative person with a peculiar intelligence that seeks to infringe upon the established inhuman practices. Apparently, he tries to hunt new ways of life, which suit his personality as a man having his own 'voice'. He doesn't like his father's subservient nature and the latter's mortgaging his life to the touchables' service. Thus, his father, who stands for tradition, always doubts his son's rebellious nature. The interaction between father and son reveals their different identities; the son follows modernity, whereas his father sticks to his old tradition:

> Vellaya Pappen feared for his younger son. He couldn't say what it was that frightened him. It was no nothing he had said. Or done. It was not what he said, but the way he said it. Now what he did, but the way he did it. (76)

His father doesn't like his son's silent way of revolting, because he has accepted the relevance of upper class tradition and helplessly accepts its inhuman authority and discrimination. On the contrary, his son tries to create history by quietly challenging the orthodoxy of a caste-ridden society. In the eyes of the society, Velutha is not only economically poor but socially, culturally and mentally as well. He is insecure in the castle of his skin. So he joins the communist party and intentionally makes an attempt to wash out his lower caste identity. But the party betrays him. Perhaps, more than the party, it is Ammu who shares the social aspirations of Velutha. Hence, he is willing to join hands with her in her revolt against the social and sexual norms of the dominant groups. Man-made distinctions and divisions on the basis of colour, caste and birth are always hazardous for social harmony, peace and unity. Any form of suppression will have dangerous repercussions. Ammu and Velutha, heralds of social equality, make an earnest effort to bridge the gap between touchables and untouchables.

Both of them are aware of the consequences of their revolt and they are ready to face them: "They looked at each other. They weren't thinking any more. The time for that had come and gone. Smashed smiles lay ahead of them. But that would be better" (334).

Their deaths imply the fact that for the establishment of real multiculturalism in a postcolonial society, one has to make 'bloody' sacrifices. Conventional forms of multiculturalism, in a sense, promoted cultural demarcations. But the attempt of Ammu and Velutha is to cross the barriers of multiculturalism and to see if human beings can live together as human beings connected by the bond of love. If at all such coexistence is impossible, Roy seems to argue, multiculturalism should not impose barriers on the sexual aspirations of people belonging to diverse cultures/castes.

Velutha's attempt to eat the 'forbidden fruit' disturbs the so-called custodians of mainstream culture, but he doesn't bother about the consequences of his act. When he meets Ammu on the bank of a river, he forgets his culture, caste and origin and prepares himself for facing further consequences:

> She put her arms around him. He tried to be rational: what's the worst thing than can happen? I could lose everything. My job. My family. My livelihood. Everything. (334)

Velutha's fortitude in violating the social and communal boundaries carries the positive meaning that the postmodern youth is bold enough to break the traditional ways of discrimination and inequality in the name of culture and caste. Velutha doesn't bother about his origin as untouchable and works diligently in the factory. But his upper caste fellow workers always feel envious of his skills and competence and treat him as an 'outcaste'. In fact, he tries to establish a peaceful coexistence with his fellow workers but his stigma of untouchability pushes him back and puts him in trouble. As P.S. Ramana (2006: 226) views: "The novel particularly exposes the caste/class based, gendered and biased social system manifestly operational, in Indian society that gives privilege to the higher castes, upper classes over lower castes, poor classes and women."

Velutha, a man of self-respect, doesn't repent his sexual relations with Ammu. When he comes to know that his affair with Ammu is disclosed by his father, without any apprehension, he approaches Mammachi, though she insults him and calls him a 'Pariah Dog'. In her outrage, Mammachi uses foul language:

> Out! She had screamed, eventually. 'If I find you on my property tomorrow I'll have you castrated like the pariah dog that you are! I'll have you killed!'
>
> 'We'll see about that,' Velutha said quietly. (284)

Here, Velutha is fully prepared to face the consequences of his caste-violating sexual act. In the above expression, an utterance 'we'll see about that' signifies Velutha's anti-colonial voice of challenging the upper caste hegemony. He never gives up his courage, though he knows that his life is in danger. He is almost guiltless in his affair with Ammu, but touchables make him the villain of the 'drama' and put him to death. It is an irony that his father discloses the transgression of his son who tries to bridge the age-old gap between the touchable and untouchable: "He offered to kill his son with his bare hands. To destroy what he had created" (78).

It doesn't mean that his father is resentful to his son, but he is a passive sufferer of caste and class hegemony which is more domineering even in postmodern India. On the contrary, his son, a rebel, challenges the deep-rooted caste and class hegemony and makes an earnest effort to create his new subculture. Vellaya Pappen and Velutha stand in opposite positions; one stands for tradition accepting caste-based discrimination as the will of God, whereas the other represents the postmodern youth who tries to give 'voice' to the 'voiceless' and strive for a new social order which is quite natural. And it is quite natural that he gets no support from any corner of society because of the caste and class ridden social structure of India. However, what is significant is Ammu and Velutha's reluctance to yield to the old world and the desire for social change, though they knew the consequences. In this respect, Umed Singh (2006: 88) says: "His victimization and marginalisation begins the day when he was born in an untouchable caste. As he grows up into a young man, he does not seem to toe the line of his father, a typical untouchable who accepts the caste-based discrimination as the will of God." Velutha tries to live a dignified life but he becomes the victim of the collective hatred of caste, class, culture, history and politics. All have conspired against him. Velutha's character underlines the fact that physical power always remains powerless before the inhuman strength of the caste and class hegemony of India.

There are different instances of Velutha's victimization on the ground of his low caste origin. For instance, when Mammachi rehires him as a carpenter in the factory, upper caste workers start buzzing against him and argue that Paravans are not to be rehired as carpenters, because carpentry is not their ancestor's profession. They are only made for menial work. Velutha's caste restricts him and makes him socially weak. So he tries to wash out his caste stigma by continuing his relations with a willing Ammu, who shares his perception. Velutha doesn't get the fruits of his talent in the factory because of his caste. When Velutha finds himself in his hours of turmoil, he immediately approaches Comrade Pillai for support but Pillai remains cool and unkind to Velutha, because he knows that Velutha is a Paravan not to be supported. In this respect, Shyam S. Agarwalla (1999: 274) views: "Roy is determined to expose the hypocrisy of the upper caste communists, the dominant group who talk of casteless and classless society, and raise slogans for the unity of all working class people." It is an irony that on the one hand, Communists fight for a casteless, classless and exploitation-free society, but on the other hand feudal lords like Pillai promote all social evils including casteism. He calls Velutha 'a Paravan' and warns Chacko about him because Velutha is a card-holding member of the party. Velutha's affair with Ammu shocks the upper caste people who are very much caste conscious. Pillai's cool but his hideous attitude and acts show that he is not different from them.

Velutha also becomes a victim of power politics. Comrade Pillai spoils Velutha's image before factory workers, because he knows that day-by-day Velutha is emerging as a devoted Marxist leader who would be a threat to him. So Pillai deliberately pushes him away and makes his political way hurdle-free. In the eyes of Comrade Pillai, Velutha is an emerging enemy. So he waits for an opportunity to remove him from his political path of progress. But he never comes out openly against Chacko whom he always refers to as 'the management' because he wants to run his printing press with his support. Indeed, all his political strategies and steps are against the principles of Communism but he is a skilled 'omletter'. Velutha becomes a victim of Comrade Pillai's anti-human political ideology and his shrewdness.

Roy directs her anger not only at the politicians, but also at the police who advertise themselves for Politeness, Obedience, Loyalty, Intelligence, Courtesy and Efficiency. When Baby Kochamma misrepresents Velutha's case in the police station, Inspector Thomas Mathew decides to deal with the case politically, because he is of the Congress Party. He also gets in touch with Comrade Pillai: "They were not friends, Comrade Pillai and Inspector Thomas Mathew, and they didn't trust each other. But they understood each other perfectly.... They were mechanics who serviced different parts of the machine" (264).

After confirming Velutha's case from Comrade Pillai, without any delay, he arrests Velutha and brutally kills him in the police station. Roy exposes the brutish power of the police force, which maintains its political interest, while it handles different cases, related to caste, religion or any political parties. Velutha's case is 'properly' handled by the alliance between politics (Communism) and police (Congress). The fact is, Velutha is not the victim of any single force but of many forces like caste discrimination, dirty politics and a rabid police force.

'Colonialism' is a relatively new theory but its practical applications have been in India for a long time. India is still a colonizers' land where the so-called upper caste elites exploit the underprivileged classes and make them more fragile. It means colonialism in India is still breathing, although it is 'Home Colonialism'. Roy directly expresses her anger against the colonial mentality of the upper caste people who are not in a position to accept change, because of their misconceptions and prejudice against caste, culture and community. They are very much against the minority cultures and for their exclusive existence.

Accommodating and accepting different cultures, subcultures, castes and communities along with their varied hues and tastes is now the basic need of a postmodern world, because each culture or subculture has its own set of values and norms. Irrespective of culture, subculture, caste and community, every individual has his/her own birthright to enjoy his/her free life, because life is only a single gift equally given by God to all human beings. So giving respect to each other's culture means giving respect to each individual, because every individual is a product of his culture. By handling the theme of an inter caste love affair, Roy tries to highlight the need of a casteless and peaceful society where everybody's interest should be protected and respected for strengthening the principles of democratic multiculturalism. Velutha's anti-colonial voice, though defeated, definitely conveys a message to the postmodern society, that, time has come to accept the fact of social heterogeneity because everybody is now very much conscious about his/her caste, culture and religious identities which are more or less equally valuable. If we disrespect any culture or caste, it will lead to conflict and social unrest. Therefore, in the postmodern world, identity recognition and recognition of differences becomes the lifeline of multicultural societies like India. Velutha's act of entering into the 'prohibited zone' challenges the upper caste hegemony and gives the message that no community/culture should attempt to dominate another, especially at a time when everyone is getting more and more conscious of his/her own 'space' in society. A multicultural policy in India sometimes becomes lethargic due to misunderstanding of caste stigma and social stratification based on class, culture and religion.

6

Conclusion

The present study is an attempt to explore how multiculturalism, a social theory/ideology, plays a vital role in literary studies. Multiculturalism challenges a monoculture society and celebrates cultural pluralism. The coexistence of numerous cultures and subcultures can develop a healthy human society characterized by co-operation, tolerance, respect and love. The idea of preserving all cultures is a way of recognizing different cultures and representing them as equals in the public arena. The preservation of different cultures leads towards the integrity and truthfulness of society. Multiculturalism opposes cultural hegemony and appreciates cultural diversity and respects the notion of multiple identities. It recognizes and respects minority cultures that have been suffering because of social injustice, exclusion, marginalisation, dispossession, dislocation and social discrimination. It explores the possibilities of breaking down inter-ethnic, inter-racial discriminatory attitudes and cultural jealousies and supports the maintenance of social harmony and mutual acceptance of all cultures. Therefore, in the present study, an attempt is made to look at multiculturalism from sociological perspectives.

For a theoretical background different views and opinions of various social scientists, philosophers and political thinkers have been considered and discussed. The sociological facet of multiculturalism in the present study includes harmonious coexistence of multiple cultures and subcultures, value of tolerance (non-discriminatory attitude), privileges and protection to minority cultures, importance of cultural, religious and ethnic diversities, significance of cultural, communal, ethnic and religious identities.

After an extensive theoretical survey of multiculturalism and its different forms, an attempt is made to focus on some of its negative aspects and dark sides also. The background closes with a detailed survey of Indian multiculturalism, as it is reflected/deflected in the works of some Indian novelists in English. To get acquainted with Indian multiculturalism, an attempt is made to trace the social, cultural and religious history of India. Though Indian society is divided on the basis of religion, caste and class, Indian Constitution has played a vital role in promoting the value of multiculturalism, a social theory of integrating people of diverse religions, cultures and backgrounds. Theoretical framework ends with an explanation as how Indian multiculturalism maintains its accommodativeness and accepts originality of cultures.

Another concern of the thesis is to study the history of Indian society where caste was a major hurdle in the progress of the untouchables. For this purpose, Mulk Raj Anand's *Untouchable* is taken as a case in point. Bakha, the protagonist of the novel, suffers a lot because of caste stigma, poverty, oppression, social injustice and exploitation. He has a burning desire to protest against the caste Hindus, the members of the mainstream dominant culture, but fails in his mission of forming an egalitarian society, because of his weak will. In *Untouchable*, we notice cultural diversity without respect and peaceful coexistence. A rift between the dominant and subordinate cultures is visible which has advanced social disharmony and discord in the village. The sharp division of the multicultural village, along the lines of caste and occupation shows the institutionalized social disharmony and inequality reinforced by the caste system in India. Multiculturalism recognizes cultural diversity and appreciates the value of tolerance. It encourages the principles of social equality and non-discrimination and welcomes the idea of inclusiveness. It also acknowledges horizontal coexistence of diverse cultures with mutual respect and helps to erode the dominance of one culture over the others. But in the novel, the principles of multiculturalism are violated because of the rigidity of the Indian caste system, which has divided people on the basis of colour, occupation, and the wrong notions of purity and pollution. Mulk Raj Anand has depicted the social reality of Hindu society in which a group of untouchables are deprived of their basic human rights and needs. As a social doctrine, multiculturalism strengthens democratic principles which ensure that every citizen has equal rights and that he is entitled to the same kind of protection and opportunity. But in the novel, the untouchables are cunningly and cleverly sidetracked by the so-called dominant culture, a controller of social power structures. The dominant culture has exploited and disrespected the subordinate cultures and managed to establish its cultural hegemony and control. As a result, the marginalized groups, especially the untouchables have started demanding equality, one of the principles of multiculturalism that is violated in the novel. Though multiculturalism seeks special privileges and protections to the minority or subordinate cultures, Bakha, the representative of minority cultures remains helpless and inactive because the pressure and force of dominant culture overwhelms him.

Throughout the novel, Mulk Raj Anand has exposed the helplessness of minority cultures that have been deprived and depressed due to different reasons. The dominant culture's social control over power structures, he seems to argue, remains constant in India. By promoting wrong notions like purity, impurity or pollution, the dominant culture has exploited the minority cultures and deprived them of their social, cultural, economic and political rights. Hence, Indian caste system is one of the major forces that has fostered cultural dominance, exploitation, social inequality, injustice, racial discrimination, socio-economic marginalisation, intolerance and subordination of minority cultures. Bakha, the protagonist of the novel is rolled through shocking experiences throughout the day and at the end of the day he is left to console himself with the awareness that all social problems are deep rooted in the Indian caste system that has deprived minority cultures of their basic human rights. By depicting the social reality of Indian society, Mulk Raj Anand has rightly exposed the rift between the dominant and subordinate/minority cultures. Therefore, at present, Indian constitution, an important document of multiculturalism, is only a source of comfort to the minority cultures.

The impact of partition in the history of India before 1947 and after it constitutes a major theme of this thesis. The example taken for exploring the theme is Khushwant Singh's *Train to Pakistan*. For the sake of interpretative convenience, the novel is analyzed along two separate lines. The first line involves a pre-partition period in which the principles of multiculturalism are positively and clearly reflected, whereas, the second line focuses on the post-partition period in the novel which has brought in discrimination, dislocation, displacement, disintegration, doubt, hatred and loss of human values. In *Train to Pakistan*, Khushwant Singh has tried to unlock the history of India's partition and its horrifying consequences at all levels—religious, cultural, social and political. In pre-partition period, the Sikhs, Hindus, and Muslims in Mano Majra have made a positive contribution to solidify a cultural mosaic in Punjab. Different cultural and religious groups were free to define their own ways of life. They could enjoy their religious, cultural and linguistic practices and customary ways. They respected each other's religion and culture and encouraged differences in food habits, lifestyles, beliefs and different cultural and religious practices. In a sense, all communities and cultures were quite accommodative and open to accept the fact of social heterogeneity, one of the principles of multiculturalism. In fact, there was no inequality and disparity between the majority and minority. They valued the principles of multiculturalism by respecting 'differences'. They respected differences in terms of culture, religion, ideology, way of thinking, feeling, lifestyle, dress codes, habits and so on. This kind of socio-cultural diversity encouraged a healthy competition between them. Their harmonious social co-existence is a real illustration of a slogan of multiculturalism, i.e. 'Living together separately'.

However, the second line of analysis focuses on the evil consequences of partition. Though partition is a political decision taken by the so-called leaders on the basis of religion, it has disturbed and troubled the peaceful coexistence of masses. Multiculturalism, a social ideology gets disrupted because of the decision of partition. The people of all communities and religions have previously fostered and cultivated the idea of multiculturalism, but partition makes them culturally and socially separate. This also indicates the negative impact of partition on the lives of innocent and ordinary people. Partition only makes their lives more insecure and anxious. The masses of diverse cultures, different communities and religions of India have always tried to maintain socio-cultural harmony and religious diversity. But partition was a blow to their attempt to safeguard socio-cultural harmony and religious diversity. Partition creates waves of communal hatred and disharmony in different parts of the country. In fact, common people were not happy with the political decision of partition, which had permanently dislocated and displaced them from their soil and socio-cultural harmony. The stormy rumours of atrocities committed by the Sikhs on Muslims and the Muslims on Sikhs spoil the peaceful atmosphere of the village. As a result, social peace, integrity, tranquility and harmony of Mano Majra get disrupted. Before partition, there was no social friction or conflict between two communities on the basis of their numerical strength—majority and minority. Both the communities have maintained their healthy relations based on equality, love, tolerance, respect, recognition and value to social, cultural and religious diversity. But partition has fractured their age-old socio-cultural, socio-religious and socio-communal harmony. In a sense, Sikh-Muslim emotional integrity is a sign of respect and tolerance to each other's religion and culture. But partition makes them leave their hometown with tears in their eyes. This is how partition gives birth to miseries, sufferings and develops a sense of cultural rootlessness among the people. In pre-partition Punjab, Sikhs and Muslims have consciously formed and maintained a stable multicultural society, based on the principles of multiculturalism, i.e. peaceful co-existence, equal respect to cultural plurality, religious diversity, recognition of differences, communal harmony, mutual trust, cultural tolerance and freedom to enjoy distinctive ways of life. In a sense, in pre-partition Punjab, all communities, irrespective of their culture and religion, were enjoying the fruits of multiculturalism. But partition dislocates and uproots them from their soil of birth and growth.

The manifestations of multiculturalism abroad and how they affect Indian immigrants are two ideas explored here with reference to Anita Desai's *Bye Bye Blackbird*. The Indian immigrants' problem of acculturation is an important theme of the novel. In the process of acculturation, there is a continuous dominance of the Occidental culture over the Oriental. That dominance leads to social disharmony, cultural shocks, unrest and friction. Desai presents blackbirds (Indian Immigrants) as marginalized, dislocated, rejected and unwanted foreigners staying in an alien land. The feelings of alienation, emptiness and barrenness perturb the immigrants. Throughout the novel, *Bye Bye Blackbird*, we see continuous shifts of ideas in the minds of different characters. Thus the analysis of the novel brings to focus Adit's fascination for and disregard to Occidental culture, Dev's disregard to Occidental culture, Europe's racial discrimination, cultural intolerance, problems of inter-racial marriage, identity crisis, social ostracization, marginalisation, cultural rootlessness, socio-cultural conflicts, acceptance, rejection, adjustment and oscillation between Oriental and Occidental culture.

Adit's inter-racial marriage to Sarah, an English woman, invites clashes between two cultures, i.e. Occidental and Oriental. Dev, Adit's friend, is also disturbed by the British people's prejudiced manners and racial discrimination against the Asian immigrants. In the beginning, Adit is fascinated by the British culture. His fascination for British culture reveals his colonial hangover which values and respects British culture. But his fascination for British culture remains fresh only till the middle of the novel. First of all, he enjoys the life of a bourgeois in England, which offers him a carefree living. For him, England is a symbol of refinement and sophistication. Adit's fascination for British culture is not so objectionable, but the way he looks at his 'home' culture is not acceptable in the light of the theory of multiculturalism, because multiculturalism acknowledges cultural equality and denounces the dominance of one culture over the other. Multiculturalism, a social doctrine, encourages cultural plurality and social heterogeneity but discourages cultural hegemony, governance and dominance. In the beginning, Adit appreciates and accepts the dominance of white culture and disregards his home culture. Actually adopting, valuing or respecting another culture is not against the principles of multiculturalism, but it is necessary to look at all the cultures, whether home or alien, from the perspectives of equality and mutual respect. Initially, he admires the history and poetry of the West and forgets the fact that the British have used them to play up their hegemony and maintain their central position at a global level. But in the end, his fascination for British culture is replaced by an intense dislike for it. When he realizes that British culture itself is discriminatory and biased, he shifts his conviction from Occidental to Oriental (home) culture.

Anita Desai does not wish to suggest that multiculturalism is impossible in England. The activities of Emma, an English lady, illustrate this fact. She respects the value of Indian spirituality and decides to form a little India club. Emma makes an attempt to recognize the value of another culture—the culture of a former colony of her own imperialist country. We come across different instances through which Anita Desai underscores the greatness of multiculturalism. She seems to assert that multiculturalism is possible only when the parties involved have the readiness to forget and forgive. She believes that multiculturalism is breathing in India, because India has maintained, at least to some extent, the balance of cultures, religions, sects, beliefs and opinions. Shedding of ego, adjustment with unknown setups and respecting others' sentiments are the essential factors that have contributed to the continued existence of multiculturalism. Multiculturalism does not only support to the cultural pluralism but also respects uniqueness and distinctiveness of each culture. The cultural clashes have no place on the agenda of multiculturalism. Therefore, the analytical study of this novel shows how multiculturalism functions in different forms to resolve some socio-cultural problems that create waves of friction and hostility in the world.

A more revolutionary form of multiculturalism is found in Arundhati Roy's *The God of Small Things*. It is essentially the story of men and women who have been neglected at the 'margins' of society and have to pay a heavy price for being born either an untouchable or a woman. Ammu, the heroine of the novel, is a representative character in a typical patriarchal society. She is not allowed to pursue her studies because of the preconceived patriarchal notions against women. Indeed, multiculturalism demands equal opportunities for all cultures, castes, communities and genders. But Ammu didn't get chance to continue her education like her brother, Chacko, who is free to enjoy all the privileges within and outside the family. Here, the principle of equal opportunity is violated by the dominant patriarchal culture. In fact, all cultures are valuable, but the validity and authenticity of each culture depends on how much that culture protects and projects the basic human rights, irrespective of gender, caste and class. Ammu is the victim of injustice, exclusion, marginalisation, dispossession and gender discrimination, because the male oppressors have blindly maintained the dead conventions and wrinkle-old cultures without any human considerations. Roy has demonstrated the biased patriarchal mentality, which has deliberately promoted the politics of difference in gender and derecognized minority cultures that are just handy cards for playing the politics of power. Though the politics of difference is one of the principles of multiculturalism, in the novel, gender, caste, culture and religious differences are used for unmasking the male dominated society's craze for marginalization and exclusion.

Ammu is not the victim of a single force but of forces like old value system, patriarchy, caste/class antagonism, gender discrimination, culture, religion, politics, judiciary and especially her blood relations. As breakers of 'Love Laws',

Ammu and her lover, Velutha, both have made an attempt to develop their own 'way of life', i.e. their 'subculture'. But the proponents and the so-called custodians of the dominant culture didn't allow them to establish such a 'subculture'. Indeed each subculture has its different beliefs, perceptions and various ways of thinking, feeling and reacting to others, but here the emerging subculture didn't grow independently. Their attempt to form a subculture gains no wider acceptance due to the brutal pressure of the dominant mainstream culture. It is an effort to establish a multiculturalism that transcends all man-made boundaries and restrictions.

As a social activist, Roy has tried to expose caste issues in the novel with minute details, but is skeptical about the disappearance of caste system. Perhaps, she wants to focus on the reality of Indian society, where the practice of untouchability exists only in the pages of the constitution. Therefore, she highlights the issue of untouchability and brings to our notice that the stigma of untouchability is still a major problem in India. Ammu-Velutha's deaths have implied the fact that for the establishment of real multiculturalism in a postcolonial society, one has to make 'bloody' sacrifices.

Bibliography

Agarwalla, Shyam (1999). "The Anger in *The God of Small Things*" in R. Dhawan (ed.) *Arundhati Roy: The Novelist Extraordinary*. New Delhi: Prestige Books.

Agnihotri, G.N. (1993). *Indian Life and Problems in the Novels of Mulk Raj Anand, Raja Rao and R.K. Narayan*. Meerut: Shalabh Prakashan.

Aijaz, Ahmad (1992). *In Theory: Classes, Nations, Literatures*. New Delhi: Oxford University Press.

Ainapur, L.S. (1992). "Abolition of Caste-Ambedkar's Perspectives" in S. Shashi (ed.) *Ambedkar and Social Justice*. New Delhi: Ministry of Information.

Anand, Mulk Raj (1935). *Untouchable*. New Delhi: Penguin Books.

Andal, N. (2002). *Women and Indian Society*. Jaipur: Rawat Publications.

Arnold, Mathew (1966). *Culture and Anarchy*. Cambridge: Cambridge University Press.

Bald, S.R. (1982). *Novelists and Political Consciousness*. Delhi: Chanakya Publications.

Baldwin, Elaine (ed.) (1999). *Introducing Cultural Studies*. London: Prentice Hall.

Bande, Usha (1991). "Anita Desai's *Bye Bye Blackbird*—A Colonial Experience" in R. Srivastava (ed.) *Colonial Consciousness in Black American, African and Indian Fiction in English*. Jalandhar: ABS Publications.

Bernabas, Simon (1999). "Ayemenem and the Ayemenem House: A Study of the Setting of *The God of Small*

Things" in R. Dhawan (ed.) *Arundhati Roy: The Novelist Extraordinary*. New Delhi: Prestige Books.

Bart, Morre (ed.) (1996). *Writing India 1757-1990: The Literature of British India*. Manchester: Manchester University Press.

Basham, A.L. (ed.) (1975). *A Cultural History of India*. New Delhi: Oxford University Press

Beauvoir, Simon de (1961). *The Second Sex*. London: Four Square Books.

Begum, J. and Hariharan, B. (ed.) (1997). *Literary Theory: (Re) Reading Culture and Aesthetics*. New Delhi: Pencraft International.

Berry, Margaret (1971). *Mulk Raj Anand: The Man and the Novelist*. Amsterdam: Oriental Press.

Bhabha, H. (1994). *The Location of Culture*. London: Routledge.

Bhaduri, Seema (1999). "History, Dynamics and the Individual in *The God of Small Things*" in R. Dhawan (ed.) *Arundhati Roy: The Novelist Extraordinary*. New Delhi: Prestige Books.

Bhargava, Rajeev (2002). "The Multicultural Framework" in K. Deb (ed.) *Mapping Multiculturalism*. Jaipur: Rawat Publications.

Bhatnagar, Manmohan (ed.) (2000). *Indian Writings in English*. New Delhi: Atlantic Publishers and Distributors.

Bheemaiah, J. (2005). *Class and Caste in Literature*. New Delhi: Prestige.

Bhushan, L.I. and Sinha, Renu (1996). *Casteism: A Socio-psychological Study of College Students*. New Delhi: Classical Publishing Co.

Billington, Rosamund (1991). *Culture and Society*. London: Macmillan.

Blackwell, F. (2004). *India: A Global Studies Handbook*, California: ABC-Inc.

Chakrabarty, Bidyut (ed.) (2003). *Communal Identity in India.* New Delhi: Oxford University Press.

Chakravarty, S.R. and Hussain, Mazhar (1998). *Partition of India: Literary Responses.* New Delhi: Har-Anand Publications.

Chavan, Sheshrao (2001). *Gandhi and Ambedkar: Saviours of Untouchables.* Mumbai: Bhartiya Vidya Bhavan.

Chirantan, Kulshrestha (1977). "Khushwant Singh's Fiction" in Mukherjee M. (ed.) *Considerations.* New Delhi: Allied Publishers.

Choondawat, P.S. (1986). "Untouchability and Untouchable Youth: A Study in Urban Context" in R. Singh (ed.) *The Depressed Classes of India: Problems and Prospects.* New Delhi: B.R.

Christopher, K.W. (2005). *Rethinking Cultural Studies: A Study of Raymond Williams and Edward Said.* Jaipur: Rawat Publications.

Claire, Kramash (1998). *Language and Culture.* New York: Oxford University Press.

Corbridge, Stuart and Harriss, John (2000). *Reinventing India: Liberalization, Hindu Nationalism and Popular Democracy.* U.S.A.: Blackwell.

Dahiwale, S.M. (ed.) (2005). *Understanding Indian Society: The Non-Brahmanic Perspective.* Jaipur: Rawat Publications.

Deb, Kushal (2002). *Mapping Multiculturalism.* New Delhi: Rawat Publications.

Desai, Anita (1971). *Bye Bye Blackbird.* New Delhi: Orient Longman. (2001-5th edition).

Devy, G.N. (1993). *In Another Tongue.* Madras: Macmillan India.

Dhawan, R.K. (2005). *Multiculturalism: Canada and India.* New Delhi: Prestige Books.

Dodiya, Jaydipsingh (ed.) (2000). *Critical Essays on Anita Desai.* New Delhi: IVY Publishing House.

Dusan, D. (1994). "Multiculturalism and Ethnicity: The Case of Serbs" in S. Sharma (ed.) *Multiculturalism and Ethnicity in Global Context*. Jaipur: Rawat Publications.

Eagleton, Terry (1996). *Literary Theory: An Introduction*. U.K.: Blackwell.

Eliot, T.S. (1962). *Notes Towards the Definition of Culture*. London: Faber.

Fanthome, Francis (1995). *Selections from Nehru's Discovery of India*. New Delhi: Oxford University Press.

Feagin, J.R. (1978). *Racial and Ethnic Relations*. New Jersey: Prentice-Hall, Inc.

Freeman, Samuel (2002). "Liberalism and the Accommodation of Group claims" in P. Kelly (ed.) *Multiculturalism Reconsidered*. U.S.A.: Blackwell.

Ganguly, P.K. (2003). *The Constitution of India*. New Delhi: Ashok Law House.

Garg, P.K. (1972). *Crossroads of Culture*. New Delhi: Sage Publications.

George, C.J. (2000). *Mulk Raj Anand: His Art and Concerns*. New Delhi: Atlantic Publishers and Distributors.

Ghosh, Tapan Kumar (1999). "Tomorrow will Never Die: Arundhati Roy's Tryst with History in *The God of Small Things*" in R. Dhawan (ed.) *Arundhati Roy: The Novelist Extraordinary*. New Delhi: Prestige Books.

Gibbon, J. and Reimer, B. (1999). *The Politics of Postmodernity: An Introduction to Contemporary Politics and Culture*. London: Sage.

Giles, J. & Middleton, T. (1999). *Studying Culture: A Practical Introduction*. U.K.: Blackwell.

Gandhi, Leela (1998). *Postcolonial Theory: A Critical Introduction*. New Delhi: Oxford University Press.

Gokak, V.K. (1972). *India and World Culture*. New Delhi: Sahitya Akademi.

Goldberg, D.T. (1994). *Multiculturalism*. U.S.A.: Blackwell Publishers.

Gopal, N.R. (1995). *A Critical Study of the Novels of Anita Desai*. New Delhi: Atlantic Publishers and Distributors.

—— (1996). "From the Continent to the Island: Image as Archetype in Anita Desai's *Bye Bye Blackbird*" in M. Bhatnagar (ed.) *Indian Writing in English*. New Delhi: Atlantic.

Gray, Ann (ed.) (1993). *Studying Culture: An Introductory Reader*. London: E.A.D.H.&S.

Gubar, Susan (ed.) (1993). *English Inside and Out*. London: Routledge.

Guha, Ranajit (1982). *Subaltern Studies I: Writing on South Asian History and Society*. New Delhi: Oxford University Press.

——(ed.) (1984). *Subaltern Studies III: Writing on South Asian History and Society*. New York: Oxford University Press.

Gupta, Balaram (1974). *Mulk Raj Anand: A Study of His Fiction in Human Perspective*. Bareilly: Prakash Book.

Harvey, Laudin (ed.) (1973). *Victims of Culture*. Columbus: Charles E. Merril Publishing Co.

Hussain, Abidi S. (1972). *Mulk Raj Anand's Untouchable: A Critical Study*. Bareilly: Prakash Book.

Hussain, S. (1978). *The National Culture of India*. New Delhi: National Book Trust.

Indira, S. (1994). *Anita Desai an Artist: A Study in Image and Symbol*. New Delhi: Creative Book.

Iyengar, K.R.S. (1999). *Indian Writing in English*. New Delhi: Sterling Publishers.

Jha, K.J. (ed.) (2004). "Colonial Consciousness and Racial Conflict: An Analysis of Immigrant Experience in Anita Desai's *Bye Bye Blackbird*" in A. Prasad (ed.) *Indian Writing in English: Past and Present*. New Delhi: Sarup & Sons.

Jodhka, Surinder (2002). "Making Cultural Differences: Identity Formation among the Sikhs in Punjab" in K. Deb (ed.) *Mapping Multiculturalism*. Jaipur: Rawat Publications.

Joseph, Sarah (2002). "Do Multicultural Individuals Require a Multicultural State?" in K. Deb (ed.) *Mapping Multiculturalism*. Jaipur: Rawat Publications.

Karnani, Chetan (2001). *Eminent Indian English Writers: An Assessment*. Jaipur: Rawat Publications.

Kaviraj, Sudipta (ed.) (1997). *Politics in India*. Delhi: Oxford University Press.

Keats, Daphne (ed.) (1997). *Culture and Child*. England: John Willey & Sons Ltd., Chichester.

Kelly, Paul (ed.) (2002). *Multiculturalism Reconsidered*. U.K: Blackwell.

Khan, R. (ed.) (1987). *Composite Culture of India and National Integration*. Ahmedabad: Allied Publishers.

Khare, R.S. (1997). *Cultural Diversity and Social Discontent*. New Delhi: Sage.

Khera, S.K. (2000). "Erotic Motif in Khushwant Singh's *Train to Pakistan* and D.H. Lawrence's *Lady Chatterley's Lover*" in N. Gopal (ed.) *Indian English Poetry and Fiction: A Critical Evaluation*. New Delhi: Atlantic.

Kirpal, Viney (1989). *The Third World Novel of Expatriation*. New Delhi: Sterling.

Kornblum, W. and Julian, J. (1974). *Social Problems*. New Jersey: Prentice-Hall, Inc.

Krishnamoorthy, A. (1984). "The Ballad of East and West Updated: Anita Desai's *Bye Bye Blackbird*" in R. Srivastava (ed.) *Perspectives on Anita Desai*. Ghaziabad: Vimal Prakashan.

Kroeber, A.L. (1952). *The Nature of Culture*. Chicago: University of Chicago Press.

Kukreti, Sumitra (2000). "Love-Hate Relationship of Expatriates in Anita Desai's *Bye Bye Blackbird*" in M. Bhatnagar (ed.) *The Novels of Anita Desai: A Critical Study*. New Delhi: Atlantic.

Kundu, Rama (2001) "Redefining the Margin: Arundhati Roy" in M. Rajeshwar (ed.) *Post-Independence Indian English Fiction*. New Delhi: Atlantic.

Kymlicka, Will (1995). *Multicultural Citizenship*. New York: Clavendon Press.

—— (1997). *Multicultural Citizenship*. New York: Oxford University Press.

—— (ed.) (2005). *Multiculturalism in Asia*. New York: Oxford University Press.

Lal, A.K. (ed.) (2003). *Social Exclusion: Essays in Honour of Dr. Bindeshwar Pathak*. New Delhi: Concept Publications.

Lawrence, Blum (1978). "Recognition, Value, and Equality: A Critique of Charles Taylor's and Nancy Frasser's Accounts of Multiculturalism" in C. Willett (ed.) *Theorizing Multiculturalism: A Guide to the Current Debate*. U.S.A: Blackwell.

Loomba, Ania (1998). *Colonialism/Postcolonialism*. London: Routledge.

Mahajan, Gurpreet (2002). *The Multicultural Path*. New Delhi: Sage Publications.

—— (ed.) (1998). *Democracy, Difference and Social Justice*. New York: Oxford University Press.

Malik, K.N. (1997). *India and the United Kingdom*. New Delhi: Sage Publications.

Malik, Nazma (1999). "Indian Culture" in I. Bhatt (ed.) *Explorations: Arundhati Roy's The God of Small Things*. New Delhi: Creative Books.

Mark, J.S. (2002). *Culture*. New Delhi: Viva Books.

Martin, D. (1978). *A General Theory of Secularism*. Oxford: Blackwell.

McCarthy, E.D. (1996). *Knowledge as Culture*. London: Routledge.

Michael, V. (1996). *The Multicultural Imagination*. London: Routledge.

Milner, Andrew (1996). *Literature, Culture and Society*. London: VCL Press.

—— (2003). *Contemporary Cultural Theory*. New Delhi: Rawat Publications.

Mishra, Binod (2005). "Despair and Delight in the Novels of Mulk Raj Anand" in T. Indramohan (ed.) *The Novels of Mulk Raj Anand: A New Critical Spectrum*. New Delhi: Atlantic.

Mohan, Ramesh (ed.) (1978). *Indian Writing in English*. New Delhi: Orient Longman.

Mohanty, Sachidananda (2001). *Literature and Culture*. New Delhi: Prestige Book.

Montserrat, G. (1997). *The Ethnicity Reader*. U.S.A.: Blackwell Publishers.

Mujumdar, D.N. (1986). *An Introduction to Social Anthropology*. New Delhi: National Publishing House.

Mukherji, D.P. (1948). *Indian Culture: A Sociological Study*. New Delhi: Rupa & Co.

Mukherjee, Meenakshi (1985). *Realism and Reality: The Novel and Society in India*. New Delhi: Oxford University Press.

—— (ed.) (1971). *The Twice Born Fiction*. New Delhi: Heinemann.

Mushirul, H. and Roy, A. (ed.) (2005). *Living Together Separately: Cultural India in History and Politics*. New Delhi: Oxford University Press.

Naik, M.K. and Narayan, S. (2001). *Indian English Literature 1980-2000: A Critical Survey*. Delhi: Pencraft International.

Naik, M.K. (1973). *Mulk Raj Anand*. New Delhi: Arnol-Heinemann India.

Nehru, Pandit (1946). *The Discovery of India*. Calcutta: Signet Press.

Okin, S. (1999). *Is Multiculturalism Bad for Women*? Princeton: Princeton University Press.

Ostor, A. (1984). *Culture and Power: Legend, Ritual, Bazzar and Rebellion in a Bengali Society*. New Delhi: Sage.

Outlaw, Lucius (1998). "Multiculturalism, Citizenship, Education and American Liberal Democracy" in C. Willett (ed.) *Theorizing Multiculturalism: A Guide to the Current Debate*. U.S.A.: Blackwell.

Pandeya, P.K. (2001). "In an Alien Country: Cross Cultural Experience in *Bye Bye Blackbird*" in P. Singh (ed.) *Indian Fiction in English*. New Delhi: Atlantic.

Panja, Shormishtha (ed.) (1999). *Many Indians, Many Literatures: New Critical Essays*. Delhi: Worldview Publications.

Parekh, Bikhu (2000). *Rethinking Multiculturalism*. New York: Palgrave.

—— (2002). "Barry and the Dangers of Liberalism" in P. Kelly (ed.) *Multiculturalism Reconsidered*. U.S.A: Blackwell.

Parker, J. and Others. (2003). *Social Theory: A Basic Tool Kit*. New York: Palgrave.

Parmar, B.R. (2005). "The Unpleasant and Unbearable Consequences of Inter-Racial Marriage in Anita Desai's *Bye Bye Blackbird*" in P. Bheda (ed.) *Indian Women Novelists in English*. New Delhi: Sarup & Sons.

Pathak, R.S. (1989). "The Alienated Self in the Novels of Anita Desai" in R. Dhawan (ed.) *The Fiction of Anita Desai*. New Delhi: Bahri Publications.

Paul, Premila (1983). *The Novels of Mulk Raj Anand: A Thematic Study*. New Delhi: Sterling.

Philips, D. (1997). *The World of the "Untouchables": Paraiyars of Tamil Nadu*. New York: Oxford University Press.

Prasad, A.N. (ed.) (2001). *Critical Responses to Indian Fiction in English*. New Delhi: Atlantic.

Prasad, Hari Mohan (ed.) (1983). *Response: Recent Revelations of Indian Fiction in English*. Bareilly: Prakash Book.

Prasad, M. (1981). *Anita Desai: The Novelist*. Allahabad: New Horizon.

Prasad, S.S. (1997). *The Insulted and The Injured*. Patna: Janaki Prakashan.

Prempati, D. (1985). "Train to Pakistan: Some Reflections" in R. Dhawan (ed.) *Three Contemporary Novelists*. New Delhi: Classical Publishing.

Radhakrishnan, R. (2003). *Theory in an Uneven World*. U.K: Blackwell.

Rajan, P.K. (1986). *Studies in Mulk Raj Anand*. New Delhi: Abhinav Publications.

—— (1992). "Psychology of Aggression in Anand's *Untouchable*" in R. Dhawan (ed.) *The Novels of Mulk Raj Anand*. New Delhi: Prestige.

Ramana, P.S. (2006). "Reading Literature from the Margins" in B. Mishra (ed.) *Indian Writings in English*. New Delhi: Atlantic.

Ramkrishna, D. (2005). *Critical Essays on Indian English Writing*. New Delhi: Atlantic.

Rath, S. and Others (ed.) (2004). *Reflections on Literature, Criticism and Theory Essays in Honour of Professor Prafulla C. Kar*. New Delhi: Pencraft International.

Raymond, Williams (1963). *Culture and Society 1780-1950*. Harmondworth: Penguin.

—— (1977). *Marxism and Literature*. London: Oxford University Press.

Rex, John (1996). *Ethnic Minorities in the Modern Nation State*. London: Macmillan.

Riley, B.T. (2000). *Socio-Linguistics*. New Delhi: Cosmo Publications.

Robertson, R.T. (1992). "*Untouchable* as an Archetypal Novel" in R. Dhawan (ed.) *The Novels of Mulk Raj Anand*. New Delhi: Prestige.

Rockefeller, S.C. (1994). "Comment" in A. Gutamann (ed.) *Multiculturalism: Examining the Politics of Recognition*. New Jersey: Princeton University Press.

Rodrigues, V. (2002). "Is There a Case for Multiculturalism?" in K. Deb (ed.) *Mapping Multiculturalism*. Jaipur: Rawat Publications.

Rosinski, Philippe (2003). *Coaching Across Cultures*. London: N.B. Publishing.

Roy, Arundhati (1997). *The God of Small Things*. Delhi: India Ink.

Roy, Amitabh (2005). *The God of Small Things: A Novel of Social Commitment*. New Delhi: Atlantic.

Ryan, Michael (1999). *Literary Theory: A Practical Introduction*. U.S.A: Blackwell.

Said, Edward (1985, 91, 95). *Orientalis*. New York: Penguin Books.

—— (1994). *Culture and Imperialism*. London: Vintage.

Samel, S. (2004). *Dalit Movement in South India*. New Delhi: Serials Publications.

Sarkar, Ziauddin (2005). "Postmodernism" in V. Lal and A. Nandy (eds.) *The Future of Knowledge and Culture*. New Delhi: Penguin.

Schultz, E. (ed.) (2005). *Cultural Anthropology*. New York: Oxford University Press.

Sebasti, L. (ed.) (1991). *Quest for Gender Justice*. Madras: S.N. Publications.

Shahane, V.A. (1985). "The Novel as Realistic Epic: *Train to Pakistan*" in R. Dhawan (ed.) *Three Contemporary Novelists*. New Delhi: Classical Publishing Co.

Sharma, Ambuj (1990). *The Theme of Exploration in the Novels of Mulk Raj Anand*. New Delhi: Deep Publications.

—— (2004). Gandhian Strain in Indian English Novel. New Delhi: Sarup & Sons.

Sharma, K. and Johri, B. (1984). *The Partition in Indian English Novel*. Ghaziabad: Vimal Prakashan.

Sharma, R.S. (1998). *Arundhati Roy's The God of Small Things: Critique and Commentar*. New Delhi: Creative Books.

Sharma, S.K. (ed.) (1994). *Multiculturalism and Ethnicity in Global Context*. Jaipur: Rawat Publications.

Shukla, Sheobhushan (1987). "Khushwant Singh: The Novelist" in A. Dwivedi (ed.) *Studies in Contemporary Indian Fiction in English*. Allahabad: Kitab Mahal.

—— (ed.) (2003). *Multiple Contexts and Insights*. New Delhi: Sarup & Sons.

Sinari, Ramakant (2002). "The Boundaries of Tolerance" in K. Mahale (ed.) *Tolerance: A Golden Path to Peaceful Co-existence*. New Delhi: Books India International.

Sinfield, Alan (ed.) (1983). *Society and Literature*. London: Methuen & Co.

Singh, B.P. (1999). *India's Culture*. Delhi: Oxford University Press.

Singh, K. (1956). *Train to Pakistan*. New Delhi: Orient Longman. (2005-Low Price Edition).

Singh, Pramod (2005). *The Novels of Khushwant Singh: A Critical Evaluation*. Jaipur: Book Enclave.

—— (ed.) (2001). *Indian Fiction in English*. New Delhi: Atlantic.

Singh, Umed (2006). "Indian Sensibility in Arundhati Roy's *The God of Small Things*" in B. Mishra (ed.) *Indian Writings in English*. New Delhi: Atlantic.

Sinha, K.N. (1972). *Mulk Raj Anand*. New York: Twayne Publications.

—— (1989). *Mulk Raj Anand*. New Delhi: Kalyani Publications.

Spivak, Gayatri (1987). *In Other World: Essays in Cultural Politics*. New Delhi: Methun.

Squires, Judith (2002). "Culture, Equality and Diversity" in P. Kelly (ed.) *Multiculturalism Reconsidered*. U.S.A.: Blackwell.

Sudarshan, R. (1999). "Governance of Multicultural Politics: Limits of the Rule of Law" in R. Bhargava Others (eds.) *Multiculturalism, Liberalism and Democracy*. New Delhi: Oxford University Press.

Surendran, K.V. (2000). *Indian Writing: Critical Perspectives*. New Delhi: Sarup & Sons.

—— (2000). *New Perspectives on Indian and Western Fiction*. New Delhi: Sarup & Sons.

—— (2000). *The God of Small Things: A Saga of Lost Dreams*. New Delhi: Atlantic.

Swain, S.P. (1999). "Khushwant Singh's *Train to Pakistan*: A Thematic Analysis" in M. Bhatnagar (ed.) *Indian Writing in English*. New Delhi: Atlantic Publishers and Distributors.

Taylor, Charles (1994). *Multiculturalism*. U.S.A.: Princeton University Press.

Thanuavalingam, V. (2001). "The Pattern of the Narrative Voice in Mulk Raj Anand's Untouchable" in A. Prasad (ed.) *Critical Responses to Indian Fiction in English*. New Delhi.

Thio, Alex (1997). *Sociology*. New York: Longman.

Tiwari, Shubha (ed.) (2004). *Critical Responses to Anita Desai*. Vol. I & II. New Delhi: Atlantic Publishers and Distributors.

Tripathi, J.P. (1986). *The Mind and Art of Anita Desai*. Bareilly: Prakash Book.

Trivedi, H. and Mukherjee, M. (1996). *Interrogating Post-colonialism*. Simla: Indian Institute of Advanced Study.

Turner, Turner (1994). "Anthropology and Multiculturalism: What is Anthropology that Multiculturalists should be Mindful of it?" in D. Goldberg (ed.) *Multiculturalism: A Critical Reader*. U.K: Blackwell.

Twinkle, Manawar (1998). "The Theme of Partition in Khushwant Singh's *Train to Pakistan*" in J. Dodiya (ed.) *Contemporary Indian Writing in English*. New Delhi: Atlantic Publishers and Distributors.

Tylor, E.B. (1891). "Culture Defined" in L. Closer and B. Rosenberg (eds.) *Sociological Theory*. London: Macmillan.

Upadhya, C. (2002). "Culture Wars: The Anthropological Debate on Multiculturalism" in K. Deb (ed.) *Mapping Multiculturalism*. Jaipur: Rawat Publications.

Watson, C.W. (2002). *Multiculturalism*. New Delhi: Viva Books.

Wellek, Rene (1949). *Theory of Literature*. London: Penguin Books.

Wilfred, L. (1999). *A Handbook of Critical Approaches to Literature*. New York: Oxford University Press.

Willett, Cynthia (ed.) (1998). *Theorizing Multiculturalism*. U.S.A.: Blackwell Publishers.

Journals

Abraham, J. (1998). "A Broad Study on Arundhati Roy's *The God of Small Things*" in *The Indian Journal of English Studies*. Vol. 37, pp. 115-23.

Amin, Amina (1984). "Imagery as a Mode of Appreciation in Anita Desai's Novels" in *Littcrit*. Vol. 1, X, p. 37.

Bhattacharyya, Harihar (2003). "Multiculturalism in Contemporary India" in *International Journal on Multicultural Societies*. Vol. 5, No. 2, pp. 148-64.

Bose, B. (1998). "In Desire and In Death: Eroticism as Politics in Arundhati Roy's *The God of Small Things*" in *Ariel*. Vol. 29, pp. 59-71.

Gowda, H. (1965). "Mulk Raj Anand" in *The Literary Half-Yearly*, p. 53.

Human Development Report-2004.

Jacob, G. (1999). "Arundhati Roy's *The God of Small Things*: Humour as a Mode of Feminist Protest" in *The Quest*. Vol. 13, pp. 11-16.

Jha, P. (1997). "Greatness of *The God of Small Things*" in *The Indian Journal of English Studies*. Vol. 35, pp. 113-18.

Kaur, Gurveen (2003). "Notes Towards Understanding Culture-And Some Issues Within it" in *Edu-care: A Forum for Education Concerns*. Vol. 7, No. 2.

Masilamani, J.G. (1978). "Feminism in Anita Desai" in *Kakatiya Journal of English Studies*. Vol. 3, No. 1, p. 33.

Mukherjee, Meenakshi (1978). "The Theme of Displacement in Anita Desai and Kamala Markandaya" in *World Literature Written in English*. Vol. 17, p. 227.

Padmarani, P. (2000). "The Theme of Marital Discord in Arundhati Roy's *The God of Small Things*" in *The Quest*. Vol. 14, pp. 34-37.

Prabhu, L. (1998). "*The God of Small Things*—In Perspective in *The Quest*. Vol. 12, pp. 26-31.

Ram, Atma (1977). "Anita Desai: The Novelist Who Writes for Herself" in *The Journal of Indian Writing in English*, p. 40.

Sarada, T. (1998). "Vision of Childhood in Arundhati Roy's *The God of Small Things*" in *Critical Practice*. Vol. 6, pp. 53-58.

Sharma, R.S. (1979). "Alienation, Accommodation and the Locale in Anita Desai's *Bye Bye Blackbird*" in *The Literary Criterion*. 14/4.

Surendran, K.V. (1998). "The Untouchable in *The God of Small Things*" in *Critical Practice*. Vol. 6, pp. 43-52.

Vinoda, T. (1998). "Small is Beautiful, Arundhati Roy's Universe" in *Littcrit*. Vol. 46, pp. 24-34.

Index